Y0-AGI-220

A WORLD TO WIN

SECRETS OF NEW TESTAMENT EVANGELISM

by Nate Krupp

BETHANY FELLOWSHIP, INC.
MINNEAPOLIS, MINNESOTA

Copyright © 1966
Bethany Fellowship, Inc.

*Printed in the United States of America
by the Printing Division of Bethany Fellowship, Inc.
Minneapolis, Minnesota*

DEDICATION

Dedicated to those individuals around the world whose lives are committed to the fulfillment of the Great Commission in this generation

Foreword

One of the most significant manifestations of the work of the Holy Spirit in the world today is the leadership He is giving in turning the members of the Church back to lay evangelism, to the methods that prevailed during the apostolic era.

A careful check of the fastest-growing churches in the world in any land overseas will indicate that the key to success of growth and evangelism is the involvement of the lay Christian in the daily witness, which is the primary method by which the Holy Spirit expects to propagate the Gospel across the world. That this method is effective and will work in today's modern world is unquestioned. That the Church and God's people will readily return to this method is certainly questionable because this demands hard work and dedication. It also means a complete examination of priorities and values in our lives and putting first things first. Witnessing to the Gospel of Jesus Christ was the primary activity of the early Christian.

In the light of this we believe that the suggestions and inspiration provided by this volume, *A World to Win,* and the enthusiasm with which the author, Nate Krupp, writes, may prove to be contagious and beneficial to all who read it.

God grant that there may be a turning in the churches to this Biblical method of spreading the Good News.

Clyde W. Taylor

Author's Preface

A Holy-Spirit-directed revolution is in progress! It is calling the Church seriously, soberly, and drastically to change priorities, patterns, and methods in order that a world—*every creature*—might be evangelized in *this generation.*

Much of this revolution, or reformation, centers around methods and patterns of evangelism with a growing realization that the Church must return to the *New Testament patterns*: evangelism done by *everybody* (not just pastors and evangelists), done *everywhere* (not just at the church building), and done *all the time* (not just a few weeks out of the year). It is in the furtherance of this reformation that this book has been written.

The author will be the first to admit that this presentation is far from complete. An entire book could be written on the subject of each chapter. This is, however, a booklet prepared to give, briefly and simply, a broad yet basic presentation of the personal approach to evangelism, the associated task of mobilizing the entire Church for it, and the implications this has upon the total evangelization of the entire world.

This book is directed primarily to the pastor, for he is *the key* in the contemporary reformation. It can be used as a study guide for pastors' seminars on personal evangelism, with ministerial students in Christian schools, and by the individual pastor or lay person for personal study.

Over 40 million souls will die this year. The majority of these have never heard the Gospel.

Think of it—millions of souls going to hell every year! Some live in Africa, some in Asia, and some right across the street. How much do we really care?

This book is not for those who are satisfied with things as they are. It is written for men who *want to be realistic*. It is written for men who will *dare to be different*. It is written for men who are willing *to commit their lives to a principle* which could result in the fulfillment of the Great Commission in *this* generation.

It is suggested that you read this book slowly. Spend a great deal of time meditating on the questions at the end of each chapter. Ask the Holy Spirit to speak to you through them.

The harvest is plenteous. The laborers are few. The time is short. May the Lord of the Harvest use this presentation to help those pastors who are already committed to the task of mobilizing their church in the evangelization of their community to be more effective in their labor and to motivate thousands of other evangelical pastors to give themselves to equipping the saints to do the work of the ministry of reconciliation (Eph. 4:11, 12).

Nate Krupp

Acknowledgment

I am indebted to many for their contributions to this book: to those on the Board of Directors, Advisory Council, and staff of Lay Evangelism and to many pastors and laymen as we have together discovered the truths contained herein; to Marilyn Hamlett for her thorough editing assistance; to Naomi Blycker, Stan Hahn, and Dorothy Myrick for their typing of the various drafts of the manuscript; to Dr. Clyde Taylor for his kind Foreword; to Bethany Fellowship for their interest in publishing the manuscript; and to my wife, Joanne, for her faithful counsel and encouragement.

Contents

Satan works into church life and activity a multitude of things that need badly enough to be done, but which it is not the business of the Church to do, and thus steals away both consecrated time and service from the most earnest members, who are the very ones who would be the first to take the Gospel to the lost if they were not entangled in these multiplied forms of "church work."

J. E. CONANT

Several church historians agree that the Jerusalem church membership at this time increased rapidly to probably 25,000. Some qualified men in this field believe that the number was far greater, but one thing is sure: the enormous growth was achieved through a determined, Spirit-filled, house-to-house campaign of personal witnessing.

HORACE F. DEAN

Every believer should realize that no matter what his employment is it is only paying his expenses to be an ambassador to the Lord Jesus Christ.

JAMES A. STEWART

Personal evangelism was the method most widely used by the early Christians as recorded in the book of Acts.

F. D. WHITESELL

Chapter 1

EVANGELISM IN
THE NEW TESTAMENT

The New Testament is the place to begin in a study on evangelism, for here we see the Church in her beginning and in many ways her best days.

Why was the First Century Church so successful in accomplishing its task? Is it here that the secret to success in our generation may be found? If so, then our evangelism today should be patterned after that done both by our Lord and His early Church. The New Testament Scriptures show how it was done and will serve as the basis for this study.*

JESUS CHRIST'S INITIATION OF
NEW TESTAMENT EVANGELISM

Salvation Provided

God's provision of salvation to last mankind through the atoning death of Jesus Christ on the cross is the first step in the Lord's preparation for New Testament evangelism. Without Calvary there would be no evangelism.

A Church Begun

During our Lord's earthly ministry He instituted the Church and chose and trained those who were destined to become its first leaders. (Dr. Robert E. Coleman presents a study of how the Lord trained these first leaders in *The Master Plan of Evangelism*.)

---

* The reader may be helped by turning first to Appendix 1 for a definition of certain words as the author intends their interpretation throughout this writing.

A Mission Given

To this early group of followers the Lord gave a twofold mission. They were to take the Gospel to every person in the world in every generation. They also were to disciple and bring those that responded to the Gospel to a place of maturity, teaching them all that they had been taught by the Lord (Matt. 28: 18–20; Mark 16: 15; Luke 24: 47–49; John 20: 21; and Acts 1: 8).

The Holy Spirit Sent

To this early Church, the Lord, after His ascension, sent the Holy Spirit to direct in her worldwide work of evangelism.

1. *His ministry to the saved.* The ministry of the Holy Spirit to the saved was that of preparing and directing laborers: teaching (I John 2: 27), cleansing (Eph. 5: 26), sending (Matt. 9: 38), directing (Acts 8: 29), and empowering (Luke 24: 49).

2. *His ministry to the unsaved.* In the Holy Spirit's work with the unsaved, He was to reprove of sin (John 16: 8), testify of Christ (John 15: 26), vindicate the gospel message (Heb. 4: 12), open their hearts (Acts 16: 14), and perform the miracle of the new birth (John 3).

A Pattern Outlined

The Lord not only instituted the Church, gave it its mission, and sent the Holy Spirit to enable the Church to accomplish its mission, but He also outlined a pattern they were to follow in their work of world-wide evangelism.

1. *Begin at Jerusalem.* In doing their world-wide evangelism work they were to begin at Jerusalem (Luke 24: 47). They were to *start where they were* and work in an ever-widening circle from there to the ends of the earth (Acts 1: 8).

T. A. Hegre notes that by this ever-widening circle process, the sending of missionaries to foreign nations with the accompanying task of learning another language would not even have been necessary. He says:

> Possibly then we would not even need missionaries. One convert in a foreign land would witness to another, and that one to yet another. Finally the gospel would get to the border of a country where everybody would be bilingual. Then it would jump the borders from one country to the other, and before we knew it, the gospel would be over all the world. Perhaps that was God's original plan. But the Church is so far from obedience to God's ways that we have to use another method—foreign missionaries.[1]

2. *Everybody.* Jesus made it clear that every follower of His was to do the work of evangelism. This was the purpose of their salvation (John 15: 16), the test of their discipleship (John 15: 8), and the expected natural result of following Him (Matt. 4: 19). Sin was personal, salvation was personal, and *so was the Great Commission.*

The *same* commission, authority, and instruction given to the twelve ("clergy" in our terminology) in Luke 9 were also given to the seventy ("laymen") in Luke 10. The Great Commission was given to His *total company* of followers before His ascension, and the *whole group* of one hundred twenty committed followers, not just the eleven, waited for Pentecost.

3. *Everywhere.* Jesus made it quite clear that evangelism was to be done everywhere. We see this in His own life. Everywhere He went—by the sea shore, in the temple, at the market place, through the fields, along the roads—He was doing the work

---

[1] All numbered references are listed in Appendix 4.

of evangelism. Witnessing and soul winning was a natural part of His life wherever He went.

4. *Every day.* Again we see this pattern in our Lord's life. Witnessing and soul winning was an everyday affair with Jesus as His life is presented in the four Gospels.

5. *Two basic methods of personal evangelism and mass evangelism.* Jesus used only two basic methods in His evangelism work: (a) personal evangelism—personally witnessing to an individual, and (b) mass evangelism—personally witnessing to a group.

THE EARLY CHURCH'S CONTINUATION OF NEW TESTAMENT EVANGELISM

Mission Responded To

Nothing else in life mattered to these early followers of the Lord except the accomplishment of this one mission which had been committed to them. Telling the story of the crucified, risen, coming Messiah was the *sole mission of their lives*. They *meant business* about the task. They were determined to fulfill the Great Commission in their generation.

Holy Spirit Received

On the day of Pentecost (Acts 2: 1–4) and in other locations on later occasions (Acts 8: 17; 10: 44; 19: 6) the Holy Spirit was received. Additionally, these early disciples were *continually filled* with the Spirit. They were possessed, cleansed, controlled, directed, and empowered by the Spirit of the living God. He found in them a channel in and through which He could work to reach a world that was lost. Spirit-filled living and evangelism was the norm for the day.

Pattern Followed

The early Church closely followed the pattern of evangelism they had learned from the Master. Everybody did the work of evangelism (Acts 8: 1, 4). The early followers of the Lord saw the Great Commission as a personal command to each one of them to personally evangelize. They discipled their converts so that the *evangelized were soon evangelizing.* They did it everywhere (Mark 16:20). They did it every day (Acts 5:42). They began at Jerusalem, used the two methods of personal evangelism and mass evangelism, and worked in an ever-widening circle to Judea, Samaria, and the ends of the earth.

Although the place of the local church was not explicitly outlined in the Gospels, the early followers of the Lord also saw the wisdom of building their work on the foundation of the local church. This truth was probably revealed by the Lord to Paul, for we see its practice most predominantly in his work. The New Testament is the story of the life and work of local churches (II Cor. 1: 1; Acts 13: 1; Col. 1: 2; Phil. 1: 1; Rev. 1: 20, etc.). The local church is paramount in God's methodology.

Amazing Results

Because the early Church meant business about the task, because they were filled with the Holy Spirit, and because they followed the God-given pattern, they saw phenomenal success. They had *converts every day* (Acts 2:47; 16:5), the *whole world heard* and was greatly influenced (Acts 17:6), and some portions were *totally evangelized.* A local congregation at Ephesus took the Gospel to every person in the province of Asia which is now the western third of Turkey, an area about the size of Ohio, Indiana, and Michigan combined. This was accomplished in two years (Acts 19:10), and a similar group at Thessalonica evangelized most of Greece (I Thess. 1:8).

All of this was done in a society as godless, wicked, and as anti-Christ as the world has ever known. And all of this was done without the printing press, church buildings, seminaries, denominational headquarters, the New Testament (except for a few circulating letters), modern means of mass communications and rapid transportation, or a thousand things we think we simply must have. They had none of the modern conveniences, *but they did the job.*

JESUS' PERSONAL EVANGELISM

The central theme of this book is personal evangelism. Therefore the following list of Jesus' personal ministering to individuals is given to review the heavy emphasis He placed on it.

1. Andrew, John, and Peter (John 1:35–42).
2. Philip and Nathanael (John 1:43–51).
3. Nicodemus (John 3).
4. The woman of Samaria (John 4).
5. The nobleman (John 4:46–54).
6. The call of Simon, Andrew, John, and James (Luke 5:1–11).
7. A leper (Mark 1:40–45).
8. The paralytic borne of four (Mark 2:1–12).
9. The call of Matthew (Mark 2:13–17).
10. The infirm man at Bethesda (John 5).
11. The man with the withered hand (Luke 6:6–11).
12. The centurion (Luke 7:1–10).
13. The widow of Nain (Luke 7:11–17).
14. The sinful woman in the house of Simon the Pharisee (Luke 7:36–50).
15. The Gadarene demoniac (Mark 5:1–20).
16. Jairus and family (Mark 5:21–43).

17. The woman with an issue of blood (Mark 5:25–34).
18. The two blind men (Matt. 9:27–31).
19. The dumb demoniac (Matt. 9:32–34).
20. The Syrophenician woman (Matt. 15:21–28).
21. The deaf and dumb man (Mark 7:32–37).
22. The blind man near Bethsaida (Mark 8:22–26).
23. The demoniac boy (Mark 9:14–29).
24. The woman taken in adultery (John 8:1–11).
25. The three would-be disciples (Luke 9:51–62).
26. The lawyer (Luke 10:25–37).
27. The man born blind (John 9).
28. The woman bowed together (Luke 13:10–21).
29. The rich young ruler (Matt. 19:16–22).
30. The blind men near Jericho (Mark 10:46–52).
31. Zacchaeus (Luke 19:1–10).
32. Judas Iscariot (Luke 22; John 13; Matt. 27).
33. Pilate (John 18–19; Luke 23).
34. Herod (Luke 23; Mark 15).
35. The two thieves (Luke 23:32–43).[2]

It is interesting and important to note that a study of these incidents reveal that fourteen of the incidents of personal evangelism were coupled with the masses who were following the Lord (although not always with mass evangelism) while twenty-one were separate from it. It is also interesting to note that twenty-three of the interviews were initiated by the individual while only twelve were initiated by the Lord.

PERSONAL EVANGELISM IN THE BOOK OF ACTS

Also given in detail are the cases of personal evangelism recorded in the Acts of the Apostles. As listed by Whitesell, they are:

1. Peter and John with the lame man (3:1–11).
2. Philip with Simon the sorcerer (8:9–24).

3. Philip and the eunuch (8:26–40).
4. Ananias and Saul of Tarsus (9:10–20).
5. Peter with Aeneas and Dorcas (9:32–42).
6. Peter with Cornelius (10:1–11, 18).
7. Paul with Elymas (13:6–12).
8. Barnabas and Saul with Sergius Paulus (13:7–12).
9. Paul and Silas with Lydia (16:12–15).
10. Paul and Silas with the Philippian jailer (16:23–40).
11. Paul's house-to-house evangelism in Ephesus (20:17–35).
12. Paul with Felix and Drusilla (24:24–27).
13. Paul with King Agrippa (chapter 26). Paul personalized this appeal even though Agrippa was one of the crowd addressed.
14. Paul with Publius and his father (28:7–11).
15. Paul in his own hired house in Rome for two years (28:16–31).[3]

In the author's opinion, it is of special significance that nine of the fifteen incidents of personal evangelism in the book of Acts were initiated by the Christian witness and seven of these nine were not coupled in any direct way with mass evangelism.

Questions to Answer

1. What is the mission of the Church? (Mark 16:15; Matt. 28:19, 20)
2. Who in the province of Asia received the Gospel in the First Century? (Acts 19:10)
3. What was the First Century pattern of evangelism? (Acts 8:1, 4; Mark 16:20; Acts 5:42)

Questions for Meditation and Application

1. Why did the early Church have such phenomenal success? Can this be recaptured today? How?

2. What percent of the people in your community and nation would you estimate yet need to be evangelized?
3. What percent of the Christians in your church are witnessing and winning others to Christ?

I care not how or where I live or what hardship I go through—so that I can but gain souls.

DAVID BRAINERD

We believe that the witnessing fellowship of Christian laymen is destined to become in the decades ahead the new center of vitality, power, and authority in the Church—that it will speak to this age as the Bible spoke in the Protestant awakening.

CLAXTON MONRO

You can win others to Christ, with confidence and with quietness. There may be some things you have to unlearn, and some things you have to learn. But with God's help you can do both.

ROSALIND RINKER

When the church loses compassion, Christianity confines itself to acts of worship; but when it is filled with love for a needy world it grows from worship to activity. This is the hour for action. We must take the offensive. We must mobilize an all-out crusade to win the lost. We can have apostolic success, if we follow the plan laid down by Christ. This is one task from which no Christian should consider himself exempt. . . . Soul winning is every Christian's job.

GEORGE SWEETING

Chapter 2

EVANGELISM SINCE NEW TESTAMENT TIMES

THE DEATH OF EVANGELISM

By 400 A.D., in the three centuries which quickly followed New Testament times, the Church, entangled in theological controversy, clerical hierarchy, and popularity, became almost completely apostate. For the next 1000 years God was almost without a true evangelical witness.

THE REBIRTH OF EVANGELISM

With the Protestant Reformation in the 1500's came a rediscovery of the Biblical requirements of salvation (justification by faith). With that came a rediscovery of the necessity to evangelize.

Through Wesley and Whitefield there was a rebirth of one of the New Testament methods of evangelism: mass evangelism. Since these days it has been widely used and, to a degree, successfully used.

But the Church, in the almost 1700 years since 250 A.D., has never returned to the other New Testament method of outreach: personal evangelism.

It is true that we talk about it, preach sermons and write books on it, and even occasionally make a half-hearted attempt at it. *But we have never begun to see personal evangelism restored to its New Testament place of priority, power, and success.* And there are reasons for this. We will look at some of the major ones.

Our evangelism has much to be desired when compared to that of our First Century brothers in Christ.

Mission Confused

When we look at all of the emphases, programs, and activities in the average evangelical denomination and local church today, it is wondered if we have not somewhat forgotten or at least become confused on exactly what the true, God-given mission of the Church is. *We're busy, but busy about what?* We are so busy with church work that we *no longer have time to do the Work of the Church.*

Arthur C. Archibald has put it:

> We profess that evangelism is our chief task; but with few exceptions, our churches are organized for everything except for our central project. 99 per cent of our churches do not even have a standing committee or board on evangelism. We are organized for worship, and what vast gains we have made in recent years! We are organized for music, and what splendid choirs we possess! We are organized for Bible study, with great school plants and noble curriculums. We are organized for recreation, and how our gymnasiums hum with activity! We are organized for missions, and our women's societies teem with vitality. We are organized for finance—how we are organized! But when it comes to the central project of the church, that for which it may be said, the church primarily exists, we are almost completely minus any organization, as bare of organization as though evangelism never even entered our thoughts. I wonder at times how deeply it does? [4]

Just what strategy does your denomination have for getting the Gospel to every creature in this generation? What way will you evangelize your nation in the next twenty years? What plan do you have as a local church to get the Gospel to every single soul in your community in the next five years? These are hard questions to face, just as they are difficult for the author to ask, but *they must be considered.* And *we must find answers,* because Jesus said He wanted the message taken to every creature. And we will have to answer for our generation.

Holy Spirit Grieved

With a confusion of the mission goes an automatic grieving of the Holy Spirit, for He is the Lord of the Harvest. And don't we attempt much of our evangelism without the real power and direction of the Holy Spirit?

One Christian leader recently said that if the Holy Spirit were taken out of the world, 90% of our so-called church work would still go on and no one would know the difference.[5] Is this true?

Flashy evangelists with fancy sermons and funny stories; cold personal witnessing without the Spirit's leading; special music for the praise of the choir, the soloists, and the music profession; loud, long, fancy praying for the hearing of others in prayer meetings sum up most of our meetings. There's far more of this in all of our groups than there should be and much more than we care to admit, isn't there?

When we add to all this the thousands of defeated, carnal Christians, we must conclude that certainly we have grieved the Holy Spirit.

We must "die" to self and become "alive" to Him, become His instruments, let the Holy Spirit truly be the Lord of the Harvest and the Lord of our lives.

Pattern Neglected

Where there is Spirit-anointed evangelism, we have almost entirely neglected the First Century pattern.

1. *Overseas rather than "Jerusalem."* Jesus said that we were to start our witnessing in Jerusalem. *Your "Jerusalem" is the community in which you live.* Yet there are thousands of Christians who give to and pray for missions, but have never gone across the street and told their neighbor about the Saviour. The importance of missions must not be overlooked, but neither should the "Jerusalem" responsibility.

Every year hundreds of students go to the ends of the earth from our seminaries, Bible schools, and Christian colleges, who have *never personally led a soul to Christ here at home.* And it is doubly tragic that many of them never begin a ministry of personal evangelism overseas either. Changing one's geographical location does not change one's spirituality or effectiveness!

On a larger scale, there are many local churches today with large mission-supporting programs; and while we praise them for this, many of these same churches are doing little to evangelize the multitudes of their own city except for those who will come to the church building.

2. *Pastor and evangelist instead of "everybody."* Our evangelism is done almost entirely by the professional—the pastor and the evangelist—instead of being done by every Christian.

We have brought much of this situation upon ourselves with an over-emphasis on such concepts and terminology as "called to preach" and "called to the ministry." It is true that God sets some apart to give themselves full time to prayer and to the ministry of the Word (Acts 6:4). But no one needs

26

a "call to preach"—to proclaim, publish, or make known the Gospel—for every Christian is commanded to do this (Mark 16:15).

J. E. Conant, Bible teacher, evangelist, and author of numerous books, said:

> The Great Commission, therefore, when we sum it up, is a personal command to every Christian to go into every nook and corner of his personal world, and seek, by witnessing in the power of the Holy Spirit to the Good News of God's saving grace through the shed blood of Christ, to win every lost soul in his personal world to salvation.[6]

One of the straightforward conclusions stated in the report from the Interdenominational Foreign Mission Association was:

> It was emphasized that the commands of the Word of God demand: . . . The total mobilization of every member of the church. It is not a question of a few being especially chosen and set forth, but rather that every born again person is obligated to join the army of God for world conquest. This means mobilizing all our resources of manpower, means and money for one express purpose—to take the gospel to every living soul in this generation.[7]

All Christians have the same calling—the ministry of reconciliation. The primary difference is the amount of time given to this work and the environmental setting in which the responsibility is to be discharged. The factory worker, for example, is to be a minister of reconciliation in his factory.

3. *Church building instead of everywhere.* Almost everything we do to reach the unsaved (Sunday services, youth meetings, men's groups, revivals, camp meetings, city-wide crusades, etc.) is based on the assumption that the people will come to the

church building or other meeting place that we designate.

Gene Edwards, one of the personal evangelism specialists in North America today, says that there is not a denomination in America that has a program to reach the people who will not come to church.[8]

We build a building, call a pastor, start the program, and invite the lost to come. *And they can come to us or go to hell!*

There are two basic things wrong with expecting the unsaved to come to the church building after the Gospel. First it is *unscriptural.* J. E. Conant has said:

> There is no command in all the New Testament for a sinner to go to church after the Gospel, but there are multiplied commands for the Church to take the Gospel to the sinner. . . . The responsibility of every Christian is not to bring the lost to the Gospel but to take the Gospel to the lost.[9]

Second, it is *unrealistic* to expect the lost to come to us for the message. Why should the unsaved go to the house of God when he does not know God? Why sing the praises of Zion when one does not know the King? Why put money in a plate for a Kingdom of which one is not a part? Why study and hear messages from a Book that you can't understand? Most of us wouldn't be in church on Sunday either if we weren't born-again. Expecting the lost to come to church on Sunday is more unusual than expecting the saints to be at the taverns or dance halls on Saturday night!

Because they're not coming, we assume they don't want the Gospel, Jesus, and salvation. But *this is not true!* Some folks have tried a church not preaching the Gospel and, not having found an answer to the restlessness in their own souls, have given up finding answers through the Church. Others have a church of their own and, although not really satisfied, have assumed that all churches have basically the same message and so do not look elsewhere. Some know those who call themselves Christians but whose lives are no different from their own. Many people just do not know the first thing about evangelical truth. There are those who cannot dress well enough to feel at ease in the average evangelical church. And some evangelical churches would rather that their little social clique not be disturbed by outsiders! God help us!

The author would like to very openly declare at this point that experience has proven to him beyond all doubt that the average person in America has not rejected the Gospel of Jesus Christ. *He has never been confronted with the Gospel.* And this condition exists also in other nations perhaps to an even larger degree. The multitudes of the world today *are spiritually hungry.* And they *are open* to the gospel truth if they are properly approached.

4. *Seasonal rather than continuous.* Evangelism in the early Church was done continuously, all the time, every day. That which we practice today by pastors and evangelists doing church-building-centered mass evangelism is, by the very nature of it, done only seasonally, periodically, occasionally.

5. *Over-emphasis on mass evangelism and enlistment evangelism with a concurrent under-emphasis on personal evangelism.* Evangelical evangelism usually has an over-emphasis on mass evangelism while almost neglecting the personal.

Mass evangelism or revival meetings, the evangelist coming for special meetings, camp meetings, crusades, etc., has been our most used approach to winning the lost to Christ. And there is a very definite place for it. But there are also some very serious limitations. To name the two most serious:

(a) *It cannot evangelize the world* because it

will only reach those who will come to the meeting place. The great evangelist R. A. Torrey once said:

It is a great privilege to preach the Gospel, but this world can be reached and evangelized far more quickly and thoroughly by personal work than by public preaching. Indeed, it can be reached and evangelized only by personal work. When the whole church of Jesus Christ shall rouse to its responsibility and privilege in this matter, and every individual Christian becomes a personal worker in the power of the Holy Spirit, a great revival will be close at hand for the community in which that church is located.[10]

This is especially true of the brand of mass evangelism that we have today which *requires the sinner to come to the evangelist* at the church building, the camp grounds, or the city auditorium. The author would add that some of this problem would be eliminated if we had the First Century Church's brand of mass evangelism where the evangelist at times *went to the crowds.* Modern-day examples of true New Testament mass evangelism is that which is being done by the Salvation Army and Open-Air Campaigners.

(b) *It is not continuous* by its very nature, for it requires the services of an evangelist.

Our other commonly used approach to evangelism is called enlistment evangelism. This includes enlisting people in a Sunday school class where the Word of God is taught. It is hoped that through this process they will eventually be saved. And many will. But this approach also has some serious limitations, the major one again being that you can *win only those who will come.* This once again puts the responsibility upon the lost. But the Lord put the responsibility upon us. It is a responsibility of *the Church going to the lost* and *not the lost coming to the church.*

Concurrent with these commonly used methods of mass evangelism and enlistment evangelism, we have seen very little of *personal* evangelism. In fact, *we have never really tried it.* And yet there are some very definite things to be said in its favor, including:

1. It is a very *basic New Testament* method of evangelism.
2. It can be *done by every Christian.* Every follower of the Lord should and can be a personal evangelist.
3. It can be *done anywhere.* Personal evangelism is not limited to certain places. It can be done anywhere that there are people.
4. It can be *done any time.* It is not limited to certain specifically designated times. It can be done any time that a Christian will do it.
5. It can be *sustained.* Not only can personal evangelism be done any time, but it can be done *all the time.*
6. It is the *cheapest form* of evangelism available. No building, no publicity, no paid preacher, no heat and light bill is required. All that is needed is a humble child of God with a heart of compassion for the lost.
7. Without personal evangelism we will *never evangelize the world. With it we could evangelize the world in this generation.*

The only way we can get the Gospel to every person on the face of the globe is to *take it to them.* Only personal evangelism can accomplish this. And with a revival of personal evangelism we can evangelize the world in this generation (see chapter 5).

The author is not suggesting an elimination of mass evangelism or enlistment evangelism, including their many variations, for they are God-ordained,

God-blessed, and bearing fruit. But he is crying for a *real attempt at that one method*, complementing all others, which *could evangelize your city* and mine—and, in fact, the *whole world—in this generation.*

6. *Interdenominational rather than local church.* Thank God for every individual and for every group that is even in the most meager way attempting personal evangelism. But, unfortunately, most of it is being done outside of the local congregational framework by interdenominational groups. This often has limitations in the areas of follow-up, worship, and church-related fellowship, growth, and service.

Those with personal evangelism on their hearts so often have to work outside the local congregational set-up because there is such little emphasis and channel for training and for service within it. Where are the evangelical pastors with the vision, burden, and knowledge to lead, inspire, prepare spiritually, and train their laymen to win the lost?

Improper Concepts Relative to Personal Evangelism

We all too often and for far too long have confused the mission, grieved the Spirit, and neglected the pattern. Beyond this we often have held some improper concepts related specifically to personal evangelism.

1. *Wrong concepts of personal evangelism.* Personal evangelism is one man witnessing to, praying for, and attempting to *bring another to Christ.* It is not inviting someone to come to church. Many folks know this, but their actions don't reveal it!

When are we going to learn that the majority of lost people in the world will never come to an evangelical church building until *after* they are converted?

As Gene Edwards puts it, "We must stop inviting

the lost to church. We must start inviting them to Christ." [11]

2. *Improper concept of personal evangelism methods.* Many personal evangelism texts expound a personal witnessing method which teaches that the soul winner deals with every person's problem, excuse, and difficulty, and then tries to bring him to Christ. This approach, which requires memorization of scores of proof-text verses by the soul winner, often leads to a debate or argument and therefore to a lack of fruit. It is *not these things* which need exalting. We must *exalt the Lord Jesus* and His way of salvation.

The recently introduced and frequently used "controlled conversation concept" of personal soul winning, where a set pattern of a few basic verses dealing with the need of salvation, God's provision, and what man must do in response, seems to be the best personal evangelism method for the day. Thousands of Christian people today—many of them having been a complete failure at soul winning for years—are regularly winning people to Christ with this new approach. (See Appendix 2 for a list of training books employing this new approach.)

3. *Improper concept of personal evangelism training.* This work is not learned from a book or from a classroom lecture only, but rather by this *plus* classroom demonstrations and much actual field experience led by and under the supervision of one who himself is a personal soul winner. God is raising up men to specialize in local-church-related personal evangelism training of this type. They are available to help you. (See Appendix 3 for a list of them.)

4. *Improper position in outreach given to personal evangelism.* Personal evangelism has usually been seen as a secondary method used only occasionally and to complement mass evangelism. Even then it has not been given sufficient emphasis or proper

foundation. Mass and personal evangelism complement each other—but *you have to have them both, first*. We'll never have New Testament personal evangelism until we set aside an extended period of time to major on the project of getting continuous personal evangelism into the life of the church.

If personal evangelism were correctly taught in seminaries, Bible schools, and Christian colleges to the degree that mass evangelism is; if pastors would spend even a fraction of emphasis on personal evangelism as is spent on mass evangelism; if there were just a fraction of the number of men in personal evangelism that there are in mass evangelism; if pastors would spend as much time in their annual retreats learning how to do personal evangelism and how to lead their churches into a consistent, continuous personal evangelism and follow-up ministry as they do discussing mass evangelism techniques; if local churches would give as much time, money, and effort to personal evangelism as they do to mass evangelism; and if just a portion of the time and money spent in training Christians to sing, teach, and have programs were spent in house-to-house soul winning and the discipling of converts, we would witness the *greatest world-wide awakening and ingathering* of lost souls that the world has ever known!

5. *Lack of emphasis on pastor's true role.* Many scholars commenting on Ephesians 4:11, 12 state that one of the pastor's primary functions is that of mobilizing his laity to do the work of evangelism. As J. E. Conant states:

> It is as plainly taught in this passage (Ephesians 4:11–12) as language can make it that the Lord gave evangelists and pastors and teachers to His people to train and perfect them in the work of soul-winning. . . . This defines the double work of the pastor. He is to feed his people and give

them such watch-care as will make them strong and vigorous for their service of soul-winning, and he is to be their overseer, or superintendent, in that service, seeing that they do that work and guiding them wherever they may need it, that they may do it successfully.[12]

How many evangelical pastors realize this? And how many are doing anything about it? How many are *majoring* on it? The *evangelical pastors* in North America today are the *key* to a return through the organized Church to New Testament evangelism. It will come when they realize in a life-changing, ministry-reforming way that *this* is their true role. If every evangelical pastor in North America would inspire, prepare spiritually, train, and lead his people out to evangelize their community, we would see the greatest revival ever and *the continent could be totally evangelized in the next five or ten years.*

A RETURN TO NEW TESTAMENT EVANGELISM, INCLUDING A REBIRTH OF PERSONAL EVANGELISM

The Need for a Return

Many evangelicals are beginning to see the need of a return to New Testament evangelism, including a rebirth of New Testament, personal evangelism.

1. *Our only hope to fulfill the Great Commission.* Jesus gave a task to accomplish—the Gospel to every creature. He meant for it to be done or He would never have given it. Yet year after year we get further behind in fulfilling it. A renewed emphasis on world evangelism and on the Holy Spirit's resources for this, together with a return to the New Testament pattern of evangelism which necessitates a rebirth of personal evangelism, holds the key to fulfilling the Great Commission in this generation.

2. *Our only hope to revitalize the church.* Prob-

ably no generation has talked and prayed about revival more and seen less happen than our own. Many feel the disobedience *to the Great Commission* by the church and by *individual Christians* is a great part of the reason why revival has not come. J. E. Conant has said, "Many have been praying for years for a great world-wide revival. When the Church gets back to literal obedience to the Great Commission the answer will come!" [13] Many feel that a *reformation* in evangelistic patterns *must precede the awakening* we all long to see.

Some, including the author, feel that one of the primary characteristics of the next, and maybe the last, world-wide spiritual awakening of the Church and ingathering of the harvest will be a rebirth of personal evangelism. It will be every Christian, everywhere, every day telling the message. It will be a return to the New Testament pattern. It will be laymen house-to-house and in the streets and lanes of the city telling the Good News.

Signs of a Coming Return

Much is happening that indicates a rebirth of personal evangelism and a complete return to the New Testament pattern is on its way.

1. *Encouraged by Christian leaders.* Evangelists and other evangelical leaders such as Moody, Conant, Torrey, and Graham have emphasized the need of this during the last 100 years.

2. *Counselor training.* A form of personal evangelism has become a part of mass evangelism in the recent counselor training procedures used by Dr. Billy Graham and other mass evangelists.

3. *God raising up specialists.* In the last thirty years, God has raised up groups and individuals to specialize in personal, lay evangelism (see Appendix 3).

4. *Recent denominational emphasis.* Many denominations are beginning to stress personal evangelism by pastors and laymen. Some are attempting some type of denominational approach, and a few have a man full time in the promotion of this emphasis.

5. *Trend among local churches.* A few local congregations are beginning to return to the New Testament pattern of evangelism with a great deal of God-given success.

6. *God's blessing upon.* The Holy Spirit's special blessing is upon all—laymen, pastors, churches, interdenominational groups—who are giving themselves to New Testament evangelism. Personal and mass evangelism are complementing each other. The author knows a growing number of pastors and laymen that are leading people to Christ every week. Some are leading others to Christ *every day.*

How to Hasten a Return

1. *Our God-given mission must have first priority.* We must put the task of getting the Gospel to every person in the entire world in first place. All of our praying, studying, planning, programming, preaching, teaching, and training *must center around this.* This is our primary task.

2. *The dynamic must be found.* The New Testament dynamic for evangelism must become a reality in our day. The Holy Spirit and all of His fruit, gifts, and power must become a reality in our lives. We may have different doctrinal peculiarities and terminology at this point, but *His fulness we can and must experience.*

3. *Begin immediately to re-create the New Testament pattern of evangelism.* We must begin to re-create the New Testament pattern of evangelism: everybody, everywhere, every day witnessing and

winning souls in the power of the Holy Spirit as a natural part of everyday living.

We, in and of ourselves, cannot create such a a pattern. This God must do. But this He wants to do *through us*.

Much of the rest of this book (chapters 3–5) is written to give practical suggestions of *how* such a pattern can be created.

4. *Give birth to a ministry of continuous personal evangelism.* Every denomination; every local church; every Christian leader, pastor and individual Christian must give birth to a ministry of continuous personal evangelism. Again, this is God's work, but He wants to do it *through you.* (Practical suggestions follow in chapters 3–5.)

Questions to Answer

1. What is the only hope for fulfilling the Great Commission?
2. What are some basic things that can be said in favor of the personal approach to evangelism?
3. What are some hindrances to and signs of a rebirth of personal evangelism?

Questions for Meditation and Application

1. How long has it been since you have personally led a soul to Christ? How long has it been since you have tried? Why?
2. How does the pattern of evangelism of your life and of the life of your church compare to that of the First Century? How should it be changed? How can it be changed?
3. What can you do to hasten the rebirth of personal evangelism in your church? city? nation? the entire world?

Better to give a year or so to one or two men who learn what it means to conquer for Christ, than to spend a life-time with a congregation just keeping the program going.

ROBERT E. COLEMAN

I must speak to one soul each day about Christ.
D. L. MOODY

If the clergyman is truly to be the foreman to his people, his commitments and responsibilities must be tailored to this function. He must be willing to do less than he ought in other aspects of his ministry in order that he may do what he ought to fulfill his chief task. The recovery of mission for the clergyman may mean significant revision of the priorities in his daily schedule.

ROBERT A. RAINES

If we were to take the idea of a militant company seriously, the church building would be primarily designed as a drill hall for the Christian task force.

ELTON TRUEBLOOD

Chapter 3

MOBILIZING A LOCAL CHURCH TO DO PERSONAL EVANGELISM

All of the preceding theory, Scriptural principles, and observations are not worth much without practical, detailed suggestions showing how they can be implemented. The suggestions given herein are not intended to be "all the answers." They are, however, practical principles and methods which the Holy Spirit is teaching the author and others in similar work of mobilizing local churches to do personal evangelism.

Pastor Lead the Way

It is highly improbable that a church will ever do personal evangelism until the pastor of that church first leads the way. There are many situations where there are soul-winning pastors without soul-winning people (because the pastor yet does not have the vision or know-how to mobilize his laymen), but the author does not know of a single instance where there is a soul-winning church without a soul-winning pastor at the helm of that church. The pastor *cannot push* his people into personal evangelism—*he must lead them.*

So the first step, in importance and in chronological order, in mobilizing a local church to do personal evangelism is for the pastor to start leading people to Christ.

Have a Passion for the Lost

The first, and in many ways the most important, step in becoming a soul winner is to have a *genuine, heart-transforming, life-changing, ministry-reforming passion* for the salvation of the lost.

Such a passion is God-given, but there is that which man can and must do to acquire and to keep it: *prayerful study* of passages of the Word of God which outline the terrible consequences of sin upon an individual in this life (spiritual death, spiritual blindness, satanic control, under the wrath of God), and in the next (banishment from God into outer darkness, everlasting punishment, and fire where there will be weeping, wailing, and gnashing of teeth); a life of *constant prayer,* protracted periods of prayer, praying particularly for a passion for souls; and much actual living, eating, and being with sinners day and night to see realistically that truly they are "as sheep without a shepherd" (Matt. 9: 36).

Be a Travailer for Lost Souls

Isaiah 66: 8 tells us, "as soon as Zion travailed, she brought forth her children." The average evangelical pastor today is an organizer, a socializer, and an administrator. *Where are the agonizers?* A church will never do effective personal evangelism (or any other kind of evangelism) until it sees its pastor travailing or interceding for lost souls. This takes time. Other less important things will have to be eliminated, for there is *no substitute for travail.*

Be a Personal Soul Winner Himself

Jesus never asked of His followers what He did not first do himself. So it is today: a pastor must lead his church into the great work of personal evangelism by being first and foremost a personal soul winner himself. *Laymen must see their pastor* witnessing and winning souls before they will begin to consider doing it themselves.

Become Aware of His Primary Duty as Pastor

As already stated in chapter 2, the pastor's primary duty is to prepare his people to do the work of evangelism (Eph. 4:11, 12).

Realize the Absolute Necessity of Evangelizing the Church's "Jerusalem"

The pastor must realize with all of his heart that the primary mission of the Church is world-evangelization, and the *particular mission* of his local church is to evangelize the church's "Jerusalem," the community of the local church. The mission of your church is to *take personally the Gospel* to *every person* in *every home,* apartment, and house trailer, on *every street* in *your community.*

The world will be evangelized only as evangelical congregations around the world actually take the Gospel to every person in the community surrounding their church.

See the Absolute Necessity of Leading the Church Back to the New Testament Pattern of Evangelism

The only way a pastor or a church will evangelize its community is to return to the New Testament pattern of evangelism—everybody, everywhere, every day witnessing and winning souls. The pastor must realize this and *be willing to pay the price* necessary to see it happen in his church.

Believe That God Can Use Laymen

There is a prevailing attitude that God "calls" certain people to do the work of personal evangelism and that these are the only ones He blesses and uses. This is *not* true.

It is true that the Lord calls out some of His

people to give themselves continually to prayer and to the study and proclamation of the Word (Acts 6:4). And it is true that God selects individuals to perform certain tasks; i.e., Abraham to father the Hebrew race, Moses to lead the children of Israel out of Egypt, Jeremiah to prophesy repentance and judgment to Jerusalem, Paul to take the Gospel to the Gentile world, William Carey to take the Gospel to India, etc.

But it is not true that there is a special calling or gift of personal witnessing and soul winning. God wants to and *will use every* born-again person to personally bring others to Him. The author knows many Christians who had terrible inferiority complexes and who were afraid to witness, but who have become effective soul winners by surrendering to the Holy Spirit and by receiving some practical training.

Actually there are many ways in which the layman can bring others to Christ more effectively than the pastor. (See *You Can Be a Soul Winner—Here's How* by Nate Krupp, Box 565, Wheaton, Illinois 60188.)

But they do need to be inspired, spiritually prepared, trained, led, and encouraged. May the Holy Spirit raise up pastors who see the worth of mobilizing their laymen for soul winning. It's no easy task, but the author knows of nothing more rewarding than producing a soul-winning layman.

Discipline His Time

The pastor will not have time to pray at every community function, belong to all of the civic organizations, keep company with all of the elderly of the city, be on every church committee, etc., if he is going to be a soul winner and trainer of men. The pastor must realize what is important and give himself to it.

To lead his church into a mighty personal evangelism thrust, a pastor must first become an expert in this field. He should read all that he can about this work (see Appendix 2 for a selected list of books on the subject), personally counsel with great contemporary soul winners and with those in the work of personal evangelism training (Appendix 3), and learn from these men by actually going with them and watching them do soul winning. Additionally, he must immediately and diligently practice all that he learns.

HAVE AN EXTENDED PERIOD
TO BEGIN PERSONAL EVANGELISM

Nothing begins automatically, especially when it must compete with that which is already existing. Personal evangelism doesn't have a chance of getting started in a local church situation until that church is willing to set aside an *extended period* of time to foster it. This is a period of time when all else is put aside as much as possible and the *church gives itself* to making personal evangelism a part of the life of the church.

For most churches, the period of time necessary to revolutionize the church into a ministry of personal evangelism is at least one year. It takes a year just to get started.

There is a decision which must be made. Are we going to continue to flit from one program to another or are we going to *concentrate* on becoming a soul-winning church? Are we going to develop the spiritual maturity, strength, and perseverance needed for the "break-through" into soul winning? Are we willing to pay the price of becoming a soul-winning church?

Make the Church Evangelism-centered

The average evangelical church today is activity-centered and program-centered rather than evangelism-centered. Stop and think for a minute—how are all the things that your church is doing really contributing to getting out the Gospel to the unsaved multitudes that need to hear it? True worship leads to evangelism. A good example of this is Isaiah 6: 1–12.

The pastor must call and lead his church back to its true mission. All that is done must directly contribute toward fulfilling the Great Commission in this generation in your city and throughout the world and bringing those who respond to a place of maturity.

1. *Direct the Sunday morning message to the unsaved.* Those unsaved people who do occasionally attend an evangelical church today usually do it on Sunday morning. This is the best time for contemporary local church mass evangelism. Laymen will more diligently attempt to bring the unsaved with them on Sunday morning if they know that their friends will hear a simple, Spirit-anointed presentation of the Gospel.

2. *Utilize Sunday evening to mobilize soul winners.* Your messages to the flock on Sunday evening should aim at mobilizing your laymen for witnessing and soul winning. As considered later in this chapter, bring an extended series of messages to prepare your people mentally and spiritually to win souls.

Rather than pastor-delivered messages every week, use some of the Sunday evenings to teach and train the people. Complement these messages with practical know-how sessions. Give them training in Bible study, daily devotions, prayer, personal witnessing, census-taking, literature distribution, telephone evangelism, soul winning, and follow-up.

Don't get in a rut. Be willing to *experiment*. Be *daring*. Be a *pioneer*. Anything is worth trying once. Let's learn a lesson from industry where there are entire departments for research and development. Whatever it takes to mobilize your people—that's what you'll have to do.

3. *Make soul winning a prerequisite for church leadership*. Spirituality, not secular position, talent, and certainly not wealth, is the qualification for church leadership (Acts 6:3). Make soul winning a prerequisite for church leadership. A prime qualification for every deacon, lay leader, Sunday school teacher, and all other church officers should be that he is winning souls. If the present leadership in the local church is not winning people to Christ, start by training them.

You may be another persecuted Martin Luther before it's all over. But that may be the price that will have to be paid. If that's what it takes, then let's do it. Remember, a lost city and a whole world are at stake. No price is too great in order to reach the multitudes.

4. *Make the Sunday school a direct avenue of soul winning*. Many souls can be won to the Lord if the Sunday school teacher will exalt the Lord Jesus and His way of salvation in the Sunday school class and then be alert to deal with hungry hearts immediately after the class is dismissed. The author had the privilege, early in his Christian life, of personally leading to Christ every one of the fifteen junior high school age boys in his Sunday school class.

Also, every new adult in Sunday school and the parents of every new child in Sunday school should be *visited the next week* by trained soul winners to thank them for their attendance, to get better acquainted with them, and to present Jesus Christ to them as the Holy Spirit opens the way.

5. *Make evangelism a primary emphasis of prayer meeting.* Many evangelical prayer meetings today are becoming just another service with nice singing, good preaching, but little real praying. Lead your people back to real, Spirit-led, New Testament praying. There's a place for singing, Bible study, testimonies, and a devotional, but spend most of the time *in prayer.* For a new approach try conversational prayer as suggested by Rosalind Rinker in *Prayer—Conversing With God* (see Appendix 2).

Lead your people to pray for the lost, that they might be convicted of their sin (John 16:8), see their need of Christ (John 15:26), have their hearts opened to Him (Acts 16:14), and be born into His Kingdom (John 3:3-7); to pray for laborers, that the Lord of the Harvest would raise up, prepare, and send them forth from that church into the harvest fields existing right in the local community and to the ends of the earth (Matt. 9:38).

6. *Have an evening a week for personal evangelism.* We only do the things that we take time to do. And so it is in soul winning. It's easy to think about bringing men to Christ, and even plan to get started. But you'll never begin to win souls until you set aside definite time for it. The author does not know a single church that has ever become a great soul-winning church or has even gotten started in that direction without a *definite, weekly time* for soul winning.

Set aside one day a week. This day should be as important and have as prominent a place in the weekly church calendar as the Sunday services.

The basic time for going will be the evening. Set a definite time to meet at the church. Begin on time with one verse of an appropriate song and season of prayer.

The pastor should then pair the people into teams of two. Ask who plans to go and who wants to stay at the church and pray. Find out who is ready to go as a leader and who would like to go as a silent worker. Pair one silent, praying worker with each leader. Husband and wife make the best team (with the man being the leader, of course), two men the next best team, and two ladies the third best team.

The pastor should give out the family assignment cards, giving at least 5 families to each team. There will only be time for one good visit but the first four may be gone, have company, etc.

Make sure that all necessary supplies are available. These should include:

1. Blank census cards for new homes discovered during the evening.
2. Gospel tracts to leave with the unsaved.
3. Follow-up material to give to the new converts.
4. Extra New Testaments for those homes that do not have one.
5. City maps.

Each team then quickly and quietly leaves the church, has prayer in their car, and starts for the first home.

Allow an hour and thirty minutes so that each team can make a couple stops if necessary before being able to get into a home, make one good visit, and have time for travel.

To give special personalized training to his laymen, which is extremely necessary and important, the pastor should take a key layman with him each week as his silent worker to baby sit, pray and observe the pastor-soul-winner at work. Then try to pick out some homes where the layman can be the soul winner and the pastor the silent worker. After each home the pastor can offer suggestions on how the layman can improve his work. Concentrate on a few laymen until they are winning souls—

then they can be training others in the same way.

Meet back at the church for a 30-minute reporting, sharing, evaluation, and practical training sessions. This time of meeting back at the church is important. Have each team give a brief, detailed verbal report. Those who have victories to report will encourage the others. Valuable lessons—how to improve, mistakes to not make again, etc.—can be learned by all from each report. A brief but detailed written report should be made on the card for each place stopped at and the cards turned back in. Then the pastor may want to share a final word of encouragement and challenge.

In all, the visitation evening will take from two to two and one-half hours. 7: 00–9: 30 is usually best as follows:

7: 00–7: 15   Preparation
7: 15–9: 00   Out
9: 00–9: 30   Evaluation

In addition to the evening work, a period in the late morning or in the afternoon should be set aside for trained soul winners who work in the evenings, such as factory workers who work the second shift, to go to other shift workers.

Prepare the Church Mentally to Do Personal Evangelism

Part of the preparation for personal evangelism is mental. It has to do with attitudes. Some folks do not even realize that all Christians are to be soul winners. And as important, they do not believe that all Christians—especially themselves—*can be* effective soul winners if given proper training and encouragement. Preparing your people mentally to do personal evangelism is very important.

1. *The pastor's personal evangelism example.* This will do much to prepare their attitudes—in fact,

more than anything else that can be done. The pastor can *do more* in much less time *by showing* than by telling.

2. *Series of messages on lay evangelism.* The pastor should bring a series of messages on lay, personal evangelism. There are many Scripture passages which are excellent for this—Luke 10: 1–21; Acts 8: 25–40; John 4: 3–43; Psalm 126: 6; Luke 14: 21–23; Matthew 4: 19; John 15; Matthew 9: 36–38; and I Corinthians 9: 19–22—to name a few.

3. *Films on personal or lay evangelism.* There are many excellent films available which can be shown to inspire interest in soul winning. (See Appendix 2 for a selected list.)

4. *Reading material on personal evangelism.* Many excellent tracts and pamphlets are available to direct the thinking of the church. (See Appendix 2 for a selected list.)

Prepare the Church Spiritually
to Do Personal Evangelism

Successful personal soul winning is for the courageous, victorious, Spirit-filled Christian. The pastor must provide direction as to how the people can prepare themselves spiritually to do this work.

1. *Series of messages.* The pastor should bring practical, Biblical messages on pertinent subjects such as the Spirit-filled life (I Pet. 3: 12; Acts 1: 8; Luke 24: 47–49; Acts 4: 31–33; Ps. 51: 6–13; Rom. 8; and Eph. 5: 18); intercessory prayer (Isa. 66: 8; Matt. 18: 18–20; Acts 4: 31; Matt. 21: 22; I John 5: 14, 15; Luke 18: 1); fasting (Matt. 6: 16–18; Ps. 35: 13; Joel 1 and 2; Matt. 17: 21; Acts 13: 1–3); and Christian warfare (Eph. 6: 9–20; II Tim. 2: 3, 4; II Cor. 10: 4; and I Thess. 5: 1–8).

2. *Private morning devotions.* The pastor should encourage and teach his people the "why" and "how"

of daily, private morning devotions. However, he had better first start having them himself if he isn't. This is a practice held by victorious, conquering Christians throughout the centuries.

3. *Small cell groups for Bible study, memory, and prayer.* Evangelicals across America today are finding that the practice of having small groups for Bible study, Scripture memory, and prayer holds part of the key to spiritual awakening and to growth in grace on a personal basis. (See Appendix 2 for a selected list of material available for use in such cell programs.)

4. *Weekly periods of fasting and prayer.* Set aside one day each week for a church-wide fast and prayer period. A good plan for the beginner at fasting is to have a good breakfast, no lunch, and a light supper. Spend the lunch hour and much of the evening in private prayer. Pray for an awakening among the Christians in your city resulting in a great soul-winning movement and the salvation of many.

5. *Monthly protracted prayer meetings.* At least once a month have an all-night prayer meeting for those who will gather to pray for awakening and outreach in your community and around the world.

The author urgently encourages born-again people to join with others around the world in spending the first Friday of each month in all-night prayer for world-wide awakening and ingathering. For further information on this growing movement write Mr. G. S. Ingram, Flat 5, 49 Hallam Street, London, W.I., England.

Locate Evangelism Prospects

An important part of getting started in church-related personal evangelism is to locate prospects systematically.

1. *Define an area for total evangelization.* Actually define on city map an area which the church is going to accept as its "Jerusalem" and, by God's grace, is going to evangelize totally. This area should contain approximately 500 homes for about every 50 active adult Christians. We can define active adult Christians as, basically, those adults who attend church on Sunday evening. As an example, a church with an average of 132 adults in Sunday evening service would define an area containing approximately 1,500 homes.

2. *Take a thorough census of the area defined for total evangelization.* A church will never have enough prospects for evangelism to keep a continuous personal evangelistic thrust going, nor will a church totally evangelize its community until a census is taken by the church. A superficial census will not do. It must be one which (a) gets data on every person in every home in the area of the community that the church has chosen to totally evangelize; (b) gets data sufficient to determine who are evangelism prospects; and (c) gives data sufficient to orient the soul winner as he prepares to make a return visit to any given home.

Determining who are prospects for evangelism can be done best by simply finding out where and how often people attend church. Every home that does not *regularly* attend an *evangelical* church (one that preaches the new birth) can be considered a prospect for evangelism. It is recognized that there are born-again people who do not regularly attend an evangelical church, but let's assume that they are not saved until trained soul winners return to the home to get acquainted and to find out their true spiritual status.

Census taking also provides Christians the experience of knocking on doors. This is one step toward becoming a soul winner. Leaving Gospel tracts with the people at each home during the census taking also makes it a project of direct evangelism. (Appendix 2 contains information on available census cards and booklets containing additional census-taking instructions.)

3. *Locate and tabulate other prospects.* Census cards, one card per family, should also be completed for other prospects which the church may have, such as "fringe" families, Sunday school families, people located through weddings, funerals, hospital work, etc. They may also be used for contacts which individual members of the church have, such as unsaved neighbors, fellow employees, etc. Another good source of prospects is the community's newcomer or welcome wagon list.

Have a Week of Personal Evangelism Training

An intensified, practical training session in personal evangelism for one week under the leadership of the pastor or some full-time person in this particular work will get the program started in the best possible way. Generally the training sessions will be held in the evening in order to accommodate those participating. (See Appendix 3 for those available to give such assistance.)

Through lecture, discussion, demonstration, and actual practice sessions, the prospective soul winners should actually master the fundamentals of home visitation and personal evangelism during this week.

An alternative to the one week of training is to have an evening a week for training over a period of two months. This training can be in conjunction with the Sunday evening service, the mid-week prayer meeting, or a special weekly evening for lay evangelism.

Have a Week of Actual Work in Personal Evangelism

It is *extremely important* to have an entire week of experience immediately following the period of training. This is the week when the training becomes practical in the lives of those participating in this endeavor. Everything else has been in preparation for this week. It is during this week that the church begins to return to the New Testament pattern of evangelism, for Christians' lives are transformed as they begin to live the life and experience the joy of a soul winner, and people are converted to Christ.

Have an Adequate Follow-up Program

Our job is to make disciples, not just to evangelize or even just to see people saved (Matt. 28: 19, 20). The Lord's work was established and advanced in the First Century because of the follow-up letters and visits of Paul and his assistants. This important responsibility cannot be over-emphasized.

1. *Make soul winners personally responsible.* The pastor should teach that the *soul winner is personally responsible to follow up his own converts.* In a sense, he becomes an under-shepherd to the pastor and is responsible to do all that is necessary to help his spiritual children get established during the early months of their Christian lives. He should continue to take a personal responsibility in them until they, too, are mature, Spirit-filled, effective, soul-winning Christians.

2. *New converts class.* Have a special new converts class of at least six months' duration during the Sunday school hour. This class could ideally meet for as long a duration as two years. The pastor or a leading layman should give them the Bible-centered instruction they need to begin to live a consistent, victorious Christian life. Self-discovery,

question-and-answer type Bible study material dealing with such topics as the Word, prayer, resisting temptation, Christian fellowship, stewardship, witnessing and the Spirit-filled life should be covered. Appendix 2 lists materials which will be helpful. For further study on the follow-up of new converts and on training laymen to do follow-up work, study particularly *The Master Plan of Evangelism* by Robert E. Coleman and *New Testament Follow-Up* by Waylon B. Moore.

TOTALLY EVANGELIZING "JERUSALEM"

When the pastor becomes an effective and fruitful personal evangelist, this is a wonderful achievement. It may take a year or more of diligent, consistently faithful contact with the lost. The pastor should pray for them, cultivate them, and win them to Christ.

Getting a small core of people in the church personally to win others to Christ is a second very wonderful accomplishment. But these two goals, as strategic as they are, are not enough. There still remains the task of totally evangelizing "Jerusalem." We dare not lose sight of our ultimate objective, which is to communicate effectively the Good News to *every person* in the church's "Jerusalem."

Continue That Which Has Started

1. *Pastor's example.* The pastor must perpetually lead the way.

2. *Mental and spiritual preparation.* The task of perfecting the saints to do the work of the ministry is never finished. The pastor should continue to inspire and encourage the company of soul winners that God has given him.

3. *Locate prospects.* Keep an up-to-date census

of the area for which your church is responsible. Continue to locate and record other prospects whether church-related, personal, or new-comers.

4. *Prayer emphasis.* All of church life should be bathed in an atmosphere of evangelistic related prayer. Daily morning devotions, cell groups, midweek prayer meetings, days of fasting and prayer, and all-night protracted prayer meetings should be the order of the day.

5. *An evening a week for personal evangelism.* Nothing should be permitted to interfere with this day a week for personal soul winning.

6. *Follow-up.* This cannot be over-emphasized. Keep working with *every convert* until all are mature, Spirit-filled, effective, soul-winning Christians.

Annual Lay Evangelism Crusade

Plan to have a pastor-directed annual lay evangelism crusade to expand the church's area of responsibility for total evangelization and to give intensified, detailed training to new prospective soul winners.

This will additionally serve as a review for those already doing this work. It should also serve as a period of evaluation, review, and planning with reference to your great task of evangelizing your "Jerusalem."

Additional Evangelism Projects

In addition to one evening a week of personal evangelism by pastor and laymen, additional special projects of evangelism should be periodically conducted to give additional experience to Christians and to contribute to the total evangelistic work of the church.

Projects to consider include:

1. Placing tract racks in laundromats; train, bus, and plane terminals; and other public places.

2. Tract passing, personal evangelism, and preaching missions to jails, hospitals, old folks homes, beaches, and parks.

Ask the Lord to show you the possibilities in your own community, for the list of projects is endless.

Everybody, Everywhere, Every Day Evangelism

"And the Lord added to the church daily such as should be saved" (Acts 2:47). What a church! Every day people were saved through this Jerusalem local church—some by personal and some by mass evangelism. The all-consuming passion of every evangelical pastor in the world should be that *every day* souls would come to Jesus through his people. A church started and continuing in one-evening-a-week personal evangelism and follow-up is one thing. A church filled with victorious, conquering Christians who win souls *every day, everywhere they go*, is something else. It is the latter that is the New Testament pattern, and it is this that will evangelize "Jerusalem" and will result ultimately in the evangelization of the world in this generation. Make this *the goal* of your church—*to produce laymen who win souls every day*.

REPRODUCE—MOBILIZE OTHERS

In the First Century, all the Lord needed in order to evangelize the world was one local congregation that was totally evangelizing its city.

The pattern for *total evangelization* of *any* given area was demonstrated at Jerusalem. The Lord *added* to the church at Jerusalem (Acts 2:41; 2:47; 4:4). Then He *multiplied* it (Acts 6:1; 6:7).

Then the Lord scattered these soul winners into Judea and Samaria (Acts 8:1). "They that were scattered abroad went everywhere preaching the word" (Acts 8:4), and the pattern for total evangelization was thus spread throughout Judea and Samaria (Acts 8–12).

The Holy Spirit's final step was to establish the pattern for reaching to the ends of the world (Acts 13–28). And the entire world heard (Acts 17:6; Rom. 10:18)!

When every Christian is witnessing and winning souls in the power of the Holy Spirit every day, everywhere he goes, New Testament evangelism will have been established in your church and there will be the *potential for world evangelization!*

When every Christian in the world is involved in New Testament evangelism the evangelization of the world will be close at hand.

Other Christians

Every Christian who has started winning souls to Christ must also give himself to mobilizing other Christians to become soul winners.

Let the Holy Spirit use you to prepare others mentally, spiritually, and practically for evangelism. Ask the Lord to give you one person to train. Get him studying some of the materials listed in Appendix 2. Get together at least once a week to share in discussion and prayer. Take him out witnessing and soul winning with you. Stick with one man until he is consistently winning souls. Then you begin to train another while your first "Timothy" does the same.

Other Pastors

In addition to mobilizing his own people, the pastor should endeavor to inspire and to train other pastors to become personal evangelists.

Ask the Lord to show you one fellow-pastor that you can begin to train. Get him studying some of the materials listed in Appendix 2. Get together at least once a month to share in discussion and prayer. Go witnessing together in your community, and later you can go and work for a time in his community. Continue to work together periodically until he is consistently winning souls. Then encourage him to start training others in the manner in which he was prepared.

Other Churches

Every soul-winning church should be seeking to raise up other soul-winning churches. Laymen should seek the Lord's will about training laymen in local churches and denominations other than their own. They should seek the Lord's will about moving to another community and associating with another church in order to help develop it into a soul-winning church.

Pastors should endeavor to mobilize pastors of other churches and of other denominations. They should also seek the Lord's will about being called to another church in order to lead it out into soul winning.

Every soul-winning church should pray earnestly about how their church can be a training center for other pastors, ministerial students, missionary candidates, and laymen in their section of the country.

Questions to Answer

1. What is the primary duty of a pastor? (Eph. 4:11, 12)
2. What is the particular mission of the local church? (Luke 24:47)

3. How will a local congregation evangelize its community?

Questions for Meditation and Application

1. Are you, as the pastor, the soul-winning example that your laymen can follow? What changes need to take place in your own life? What are you going to do about it this week? this month?
2. Is your church evangelizing its community? How can you mobilize it to do this? Are you willing to pay the price?
3. Are you training laymen who will win souls every day? Why not? How can you do this effectively?

Unless we can arouse our Christian laymen to consecrate their witness in a direct effort to bring their neighbors and business associates to Christ, we will have to write off as far as the kingdom of God is concerned, most of our modern manhood.

A. ARCHIBALD

. . . the successful expansion of any movement is in direct proportion to its success in mobilizing and occupying its total membership in constant propagation of its beliefs.

"EVANGELISM IN DEPTH"

Our need is an inspired leadership to show us that evangelism is the primary task of the whole congregation.

PAUL S. REES

All vital movements make converters out of their converts.

SAMUEL SHOEMAKER

Chapter 4

MOBILIZING A DENOMINATION TO DO PERSONAL EVANGELISM

The increasing awareness among all evangelical denominations of the necessity of a greater personal evangelism emphasis demands some practical suggestions as to how a denomination can actually mobilize to do this work. The suggestions given herein are those learned from over four years' experience in full-time personal evangelism training work with many evangelical denominations throughout much of North America.

DENOMINATIONAL OFFICIALS LEAD THE WAY

Just as the pastor must lead the way if his church is to be mobilized for personal evangelism, so denominational officials must lead the way if the denomination is ever to become a great personal evangelism movement.

Become Continuous Personal Soul Winners Themselves

This is the first and most important step. The best way to preach is to do. A denominational official is not really in favor of personal evangelism (or anything for that matter) until he personally learns how and begins wholeheartedly and continuously *to do it*. The traveling they do especially presents many wonderful opportunities for winning souls (the one sitting beside you on the plane, etc.).

It may seem strange to some that the author would even say this, but it's kindly and humbly said because there are all too many church leaders who are writing magazine articles and preaching sermons on soul winning who themselves are *not* winning souls.

Personally Encourage and Train Subordinates

There is also a very necessary ministry which denominational officials can and must have of encouraging and training subordinates to likewise become soul winners. This is actually an easy task since, when soul winning really gets on one's heart and in one's life, one isn't able to stop talking about it. The task of encouraging and helping others will be a very natural one.

Emphasize Mission of Church

In these last days, church leaders would do well to emphasize in every way possible the true mission of the Church—that of fulfilling the Great Commission in *this* generation.

Emphasize Responsibility of Pastor

Emphasize in every way possible that the primary responsibility of the pastor is in inspiring and training the laity to do personal soul winning, as outlined in Ephesians 4: 11, 12.

Training in Denominational Schools

Another tremendously important consideration for church leaders is to get practical personal evangelism training into denominational schools as a required course for ministerial students and as an elective course for all others. In this way, schools could actually begin to send soul-winning graduates out to local churches all across the continent and around the world each year. The author knows of one evangelical Bible school where a course in practical, personal evangelism is actually a required course for every student.

Encourage City-wide Crusades

Local churches and pastors should be encouraged to co-operate with other evangelicals in their city in city-wide lay evangelism training crusades such as are currently being held in many parts of the Continent. If every evangelical church in North America would return to the New Testament pattern of evangelism and begin to evangelize its own community, North America could be totally evangelized in a very few years.

HAVE A DENOMINATIONAL DIRECTOR OF PERSONAL EVANGELISM

Just as it is of paramount importance for all of the denominational officials to set the example and lead the way, it is also necessary to commission a denominational director of personal evangelism. His function should include at least the following:

Give Leadership to
Denominational Personal Evangelism Thrust

Coordinate and give direction to the entire denominational program of personal evangelism.

Hold Conferences with Pastors

Next to denominational officials, and in some ways more strategic, the pastors hold the key to a denomination-wide personal evangelism thrust. Many of them are very eager to learn how to become more effective personal soul winners and how to lead their laymen into this work. Two-day conferences with pastors throughout the different geographic areas of the denomination is the first step in getting pastors started.

Conduct Personal Evangelism Crusades

As soon as officials are beginning to set the pace and pastors are beginning to become personal soul winners themselves, the next step is to actually conduct two-week personal evangelism crusades in strategic churches throughout the denomination. Through these crusades, the director will give personal leadership and direction in helping strategic churches mobilize for personal evangelism as outlined in chapter 3. Churches in close geographical proximity can co-operate in a united crusade. Also, many pastors can conduct their own crusade. In many ways these crusades will be one of the director's most important responsibilities. It is these grass-roots training crusades which actually get churches started in a continuous personal evangelism ministry.

Follow-up Retreats

Within three to six months after a series of crusades in a given area, the director should return and conduct a weekend retreat for all who participated in the crusades in order to give additional inspiration, know-how counsel and specific direction. This will be a "shot in the arm" which will keep the forward thrust moving.

Introduce Materials

The director should review, introduce, and make available to pastors and laymen the best in materials for use in a personal evangelism ministry: census cards, books giving Biblical basis and practical know-how, films, New Testaments, tracts, and follow-up supplies. (See Appendix 2 for recommended materials.)

Questions for Meditation and Application

1. What can you do to help bring about a rebirth of personal evangelism in the Church around the world?
2. What can you do to help mobilize your denomination to do personal evangelism?
3. What part does God have for you to play in evangelizing the world? Are you satisfied with what you're doing? What more can you do?

Give me a hundred men who love God with all their hearts, and fear nothing but sin, and I will move the world.

JOHN WESLEY

In this day of mass dynamics and group thinking throughout our social structure, it must be constantly emphasized that our neglected spiritual resource for world evangelism is the layman who has been given adequate scriptural follow-up care. He is the shortest and most effective avenue to evangelizing the area of a church's influence.

WAYLON MOORE

Almost a million persons in the world die each week without Christ.

LEONARD RAVENHILL

Let me tell you what I believe the need of the hour is. Maybe I should call it the answer to the need of the hour. I believe it is an army of soldiers, dedicated to Jesus Christ, who believe not only that He is God, but that He can fulfill every promise He has ever made, and that there isn't anything too hard for Him. It is the only way we can accomplish the thing that is on His heart—getting the Gospel to every creature.

DAWSON TROTMAN

Chapter 5

FULFILLING
THE GREAT COMMISSION
IN THIS GENERATION

Close to two-thirds of the world's population has never heard the Gospel. One thousand tribes have never received their first missionary. There are approximately 1700 languages without a single verse of Scripture. The world's population will double in less than 50 years. We are faced with a great task!

Thirty-five percent of the world's wealth is in the hands of America's 7% of the world's population. Additionally, the United States has tremendous educational resources. It is obvious that much of the manpower and finances for evangelizing the world must come from the United States of America.

Having said all of this and wanting to emphasize the importance of it, the author, however, would move on quickly to say that basically the task of world evangelization will be accomplished only as the people of *each* nation of the world *reach their own nation* with the Gospel. The national Christians of every country must penetrate their own country.

The penetration of every nation will be accomplished as the Christians of every nation penetrate each of their individual "worlds" or spheres of influence. This individual penetration will be by occupation, location, and age group.

Let's take the United States as an example. The Christian doctors of America must evangelize the unsaved doctors of America, the Christian engineers must evangelize the unsaved engineers, etc. This is evangelization by occupation.

The Christians in the city of Chicago must evangelize the unsaved in the city of Chicago. A man who works on the north side of town, lives on the south side, and has business dealings on the west side, will have opportunity to evangelize in three areas of the city—north, south, and west. This is evangelization by location.

The young people of America can best reach the young people, young married people the same, as well as middle-aged and older folks. This is evangelization by age.

Thus, a middle-aged engineer living in Chicago can reach (a) his neighbors, (b) people he works with, (c) people he does business with, i.e., the grocer, the gas station attendant, etc., (d) engineers throughout the city and across the nation, and (e) people his approximate age throughout the city and across the nation.

This basic strategy, amplified and multiplied throughout every type of employment, every neighborhood and place of employment, and all age groups in every town and city in every nation of the world, holds the key to world evangelization in this generation.

This means that every Christian in the world must be mobilized personally to (a) evangelize, (b) lead to Christ, and (c) disciple those in his "world." This mobilization includes (a) inspiration, (b) spiritual preparation, (c) training, and (d) involvement.

Specifically, this means that every Christian in the world must be:

Taught Certain Concepts

1. The lost condition of men without Christ.

2. His responsibility to evangelize the entire world and his particular "world."

3. Exactly how to fulfill his responsibility to the world and in his "world."

4. All that God is and will do in, for, and through him as he goes to witness and win.

Prepared Spiritually—Taught How to

1. Pray.

2. Read, study, and memorize his Bible with the goals of feeding his own soul and applying the Word to his own life.

3. Have victory over sin.

4. Have victory over self—have the Spirit-filled life.

Trained—Taught How to

1. Locate unsaved individuals.

2. Contact these individuals.

3. Pray for them.

4. Cultivate and love them.

5. Witness to them.

6. Lead them to Christ.

7. Follow-up and disciple these he has brought to the Saviour so that they in turn are evangelizing and discipling others.

All of this means (a) the church meeting place must become a *"sending station"* for soul winners; (b) the activities of the church when it meets must *contribute directly toward mobilizing* soul winners; and (c) the pastor and missionary must become *"mobilizers"* (set the example, inspire, and prepare spiritually, and train) *of soul winners.*

To put it another way, the concepts and principles set forth in this book *must become a natural part of the life of every church and every Christian in the world.*

A Return to True New Testament Evangelism Imperative for Total World Evangelization

The world will never be evangelized without a return to true New Testament evangelism, including a rebirth of personal evangelism. Personal evangelism alone will never evangelize the world. But the world will never be totally evangelized without personal evangelism.

Mass Evangelism Has Its Place—BUT

1. Many unsaved people will not come to hear the evangelist.
2. There are not enough mass evangelists.
3. It is not permitted in many countries of the world—those under Communist, Catholic, Moslem, etc., control.
4. A world-wide take-over of Communism, Catholicism, Mohammedanism, etc., would eliminate this approach.

Radio Evangelism Has Its Place—BUT

1. The majority of the people of the world do not have a radio.
2. A world-wide take-over of Communism, Catholicism, Mohammedanism, etc., would close existing evangelical radio stations.

Literature Evangelism Has Its Place—BUT

1. Much of the world cannot read.
2. There is not enough literature available.
3. We cannot get literature into some countries.
4. A world-wide take-over of Communism, Catholicism, Mohammedanism, etc., would stop the printing of evangelical literature.

Church-Building-Centered Evangelism
Has Its Place—BUT

1. Much of the world does not have church buildings.

2. There is neither time nor money to erect buildings sufficient to evangelize the world in this generation by this approach.

3. Church buildings are forbidden in much of the world today.

4. A world-wide take-over of Communism, Catholicism, Mohammedanism, etc., would completely stop the use of this approach.

All other methods combined will never, without personal evangelism, evangelize the world. Our greatest need is for a great revival of man-to-man or personal evangelism.

IMPLEMENTATION

If this is true, if the Great Commission can be fulfilled in this generation through an implementation of the philosophy, principles, and strategy stated herein, then we must ask and seek answers to the question, "How can we mobilize all Christians in the world to become personal evangelists?" Here are a few suggestions.

Christian Organizations and Mission Boards

Every evangelical organization should endeavor to make the concepts and principles presented herein a reality in every local church and in the life of every believer in every nation where the organization is at work.

Pastors and Missionaries

Every pastor and missionary in the world should major on the concepts presented in this book.

Evangelists

In addition to preaching the Gospel to the masses, every evangelist in the world should begin to train pastors and laymen to do personal evangelism so that a continuous evangelism ministry is insured after the evangelist leaves town.

Bible Schools, Christian Colleges, and Seminaries

The concepts and practical principles presented herein should be taught to all ministerial, missionary, and Christian worker students. They should be an integral part of every course on evangelism, personal evangelism, practical theology, missionary strategy and methods, etc.

Also, every Christian should be required to take a practical course on personal evangelism. In this way, Christian schools around the world could be turning out thousands of soul winners each year.

Every Christian

Every born-again person on the face of the globe must become a personal evangelist and then give himself to mobilizing others in his sphere of influence to become the same.

AVAILABLE ASSISTANCE

In recent years God has raised up men and organizations who are specializing in personal evangelism and personal evangelism training work. A list of these is given in Appendix 3. In essence, they are endeavoring in various ways to teach and implement the concepts presented in this book. They are available for an enlarged ministry of making New Testament evangelism a reality in the local church throughout the world in our day.

Appendix 1

DEFINITIONS

1. *Evangelism*—To communicate effectively the Good News of Christ and His salvation so that individuals can intelligently and willfully make a decision for or against Him.
2. *Personal Witnessing*—A Christian telling an unsaved person a portion of that which he "has seen and heard," i.e., that of religion which he has experienced personally. It is usually not as inclusive or pointed as personal evangelism.
3. *Personal Evangelism*—An individual Christian communicating the Gospel (Christ and His offered way of salvation) to an unsaved person.
4. *Personal Soul Winning*—The act of a Christian actually leading an unsaved person to Christ or into an experience of salvation.
5. *Lay Evangelism*—Any evangelistic work done by laymen, but commonly referring to personal evangelism done by laymen.
6. *Mass Evangelism*—An individual Christian communicating the Gospel to a group of unsaved people.
7. *Total Evangelization*—To communicate effectively the Gospel to every person in a given area.
8. *Follow-up*—The process of training and bringing spiritual children to a place of maturity in Christ which results in personal stability, growth, outreach, and spiritual reproduction.

Appendix 2

RECOMMENDED MATERIALS FOR PERSONAL EVANGELISM

CENSUS MATERIALS TO LOCATE EVANGELISM PROSPECTS

Included are the best in census-visitation card systems for use in locating prospects for a year-round ministry of visitation evangelism.

1. "Challenge" by Barbour: Herald Press. Scott-House, 1445 Boonville Avenue, Springfield, Missouri 65802; 100 for $1.75.
2. *Census and Visitation Card*: Lay Evangelism, Box 565, Wheaton, Illinois 60187; 2¢ ea, 100 for $1.25.
3. *Census and Visitation Card*: Personal Christianity, Box 157, Baldwin Park, California 91760; 2¢ each, 100 for $1.25.
4. *Census Manual* by C. S. Lovett: Personal Christianity, Box 157, Baldwin Park, California 91760; 60¢.
5. *Census Taking Instructions*: Lay Evangelism, Box 565, Wheaton, Illinois 60187; 25¢.

TRACTS ON LAY EVANGELISM

These may be given to Christians to challenge them to win souls.

1. "Challenge" by Barbour: Herald Press, Scottsdale, Pennsylvania 15683; 100 for 60¢.
2. "Communism or Christ?" by Sweeting: American

Tract Society, Oradell, New Jersey 07649; 100 for 65¢.

3. "David Is Eleven" by Lehman: American Tract Society, Oradell, New Jersey 07649; 100 for 65¢.

4. "How Did They Do It?" by Hunter: Good News Publishers, Westchester, Illinois 60155; 100 for $1.35.

5. "Person-to-Person" by Thompson: Tract Mission, 421 S. 4th Street, Minneapolis, Minnesota 55415; 100 for $1.75.

6. "Power to Witness" by Kindschi: Evangel Press, Nappanee, Indiana 46550; 100 for $2.00.

7. "The Case for Personal Evangelism" by Lance: Department of Evangelism, Wesleyan Methodist Church, Box 2000 Marion, Indiana 46955; 10¢ each, 100 for $5.00

8. "Whose Body Is Yours?" by Wilson: Good News Publishers, Westchester, Illinois 60155; 100 for $1.35.

9. "Witnessing Everywhere" by Tam: the Oriental Missionary Society, 850 N. Hobart Blvd., Los Angeles, California 90000; 100 for $1.75.

LAY EVANGELISM TRAINING MATERIALS

Included are highly recommended materials to use in training Christians to become personal evangelists.

1. Edwards, Gene. *Here's How to Win Souls*: Soul Winning Publications, Box 200, Grand Prairie, Texas 75051, 1960; $1.00.

2. Krupp, Nate. *Bible Studies for Soul Winners*: Lay Evangelism, Box 565, Wheaton, Illinois 60187, 1964; 45¢.

3. Krupp, Nate. *You Can Be a Soul Winner—Here's How*: Lay Evangelism, Box 565, Wheaton, Illinois 60187, 1964; $1.50.

4. Lovett, C. S. *Soul Winning Made Easy*: Personal Christianity, Box 157, Baldwin Park, California 91760, 1959; $1.00 (also other books in the Easy Series).

5. Mitchell, Hubert. *Televisit for Christ*: Inter-Church Ministries, 77 W. Washington, Chicago, Illinois 60602, 1965; $3.98.

6. Pershall, Roscoe. *You Can Win Them*: Beacon Hill Press, Kansas City, Missouri 64141, 1960; 50¢.

7. Verwer, George. *Literature Evangelism*: Moody Press, Chicago, Illinois 60610, 1963; 39¢.

8. "Four Spiritual Laws": Campus Crusade for Christ, Arrowhead Springs, San Bernardino, California 92400; 5¢ each.

9. *Meet My Saviour*: Beacon Hill Press, Kansas City, Missouri 64141, 1966.

10. "Prayer Sheet": Lay Evangelism, Box 565, Wheaton, Illinois 60187; 100 for 85¢.

11. "Tracts and How to Use Them": American Tract Society, Oradell, New Jersey 07649; 100 for 65¢.

12. Cardboard Pocket Tract Holder: American Tract Society, Oradell, New Jersey 07649; 100 for $3.00.

13. Plastic Pocket Tract Holder: Lay Evangelism, Box 565, Wheaton, Illinois 60187; 25¢.

14. Sample Tract Packet: contains over 50 of the best tracts available from leading publishers, including all that are listed in this appendix: Lay Evangelism, Box 565, Wheaton, Illinois 60187; $1.00.

FILMS ON LAY EVANGELISM

These films can be shown to challenge Christians to diligently reach their unsaved friends for the Saviour.

1. "Born to Witness": produced by Family Films, 5823 Santa Monica Blvd., Hollywood, California

90038; rented for $15.00 (color) or $10.00 (black and white) per showing.

2. "Every Christian a Missionary": produced by Family Films, 5823 Santa Monica Blvd., Hollywood, California 90038; rented for $6.00 per showing.

3. "I Was Ashamed": produced by Family Films, 5823 Santa Monica Blvd., Hollywood, California 90038; rented for $15.00 (color) per showing.

4. "Just a Stranger": produced by Augsburg Publishing House, 426 S. Fifth Street, Minneapolis, Minnesota 55415; rented for $13.00 per showing.

5. "No Time to Wait": produced by Augsburg Publishing House, 426 S. Fifth Street, Minneapolis, Minnesota 55415; rented for $13.50 per showing.

6. "Seven Days a Week": produced by Family Films, 5823 Santa Monica Blvd., Hollywood, California 90038; rented for $15.00 (color) per showing.

7. "Silent Witness": produced by Gospel Films, Muskegan, Michigan 49440; rented for $15.00 per showing.

8. "You Can Win Them" (filmstrip): produced by Beacon Filmstrips, Box 27, Kansas City, Missouri 64141; purchased for $12.50.

SCRIPTURE PORTIONS FOR SOUL WINNERS' USE

These may be helpful in personal evangelism work.

1. *New Testament* (2¾ x 4½ x 9/16) good quality: American Bible Society, 450 Park Avenue, New York, New York 10022; 32¢ each.

2. *New Testament* (2¾ x 4⅜ x ⅝) better quality: Pocket Testament League, 49 Honeck Street, Englewood, New Jersey 07631; 50¢ each.

3. *New Testament with Psalms* (2¾ x 4½ x ⅝) best quality: William Collins Sons & Co., Ltd.,

215 Park Avenue South, New York, New York 10003; $1.00 each.

4. *New Testament* with large print (4½ x 6½ x ⅝) good quality: American Bible Society, 450 Park Avenue, New York, New York 10022; 75¢ each.

TRACTS TO GIVE TO THE UNSAVED

These are among the very best in gospel tracts for discreet distribution to the unsaved.

1. "A Comptroller Reveals True Profits" by Hughes: American Tract Society, Oradell, New Jersey 07649; 100 for 90¢.
2. "A Plea for Honesty" by Bright: American Tract Society, Oradell, New Jersey 07649; 100 for 75¢.
3. "A Psychiatrist Prescribes Peace" by Milkie: American Tract Society, Oradell, New Jersey 07649; 100 for 90¢.
4. "A True Story" by Johnson: American Tract Society, Oradell, New Jersey 07649; 100 for 65¢.
5. "Are You Searching for Peace?" by Kindal: American Tract Society, Oradell, New Jersey 07649; 100 for 65¢.
6. "Does God Matter in Your Personal Life?" by Graham: Good News Publishers, Westchester, Illinois 60155; 100 for 85¢.
7. "Four Things God Wants You to Know": American Tract Society, Oradell, New Jersey 07649; 100 for 60¢.
8. "Here's How!": The Life Messengers, Box 1967, Seattle, Washington 98111; 100 for $5.00.
9. "How to Become a Christian" by Ries: Houghton College, Houghton, New York 14744; 100 for $1.00.
10. "I Discovered What Life Is All About" by Hiskey: American Tract Society, Oradell, New Jersey 07649; 100 for 75¢.
11. "I Met Christ on the Campus" by Krupp: Amer-

ican Tract Society, Oradell, New Jersey 07649;
100 for 75¢.

12. "It Pays to Be One Today" by Olson: Herald
Press Tracts, Scottdale, Pennsylvania 15683;
100 for 60¢.

13. "Lessons from the Crucifix" by Wilson: Good
News Publishers, Westchester, Illinois 60155;
100 for $1.35.

14. "Ten Business Men Look at Life": Good News
Publishers, Westchester, Illinois 60155; 100 for
$5.00.

15. "The New Birth" by Graham: American Tract
Society, Oradell, New Jersey 07649; 100 for 75¢.

16. "The Priest Who Found Christ" by Zacchello:
Box 90, Clairton, Pennsylvania 15025; 75 for
$1.00.

17. "The Truly Satisfying Life" by Hatfield: American Tract Society, Oradell, New Jersey 07649;
100 for 90¢.

18. "The World's Greatest Jew, Who Is He?" by
Tulga: The American Association for Jewish
Evangelism, Inc., Winona Lake, Indiana 46590;
100 for $3.00.

19. "The Worst Mistake You Can Make" by Olson:
American Tract Society, Oradell, New Jersey
07649; 100 for 65¢.

20. "Van Dusen Letter": Campus Crusade for Christ,
Arrowhead Springs, San Bernardino, California
92400; 5¢ each.

21. "What Is Conversion?" by Graham: American
Tract Society, Oradell, New Jersey 07649; 100
for 90¢.

BOOKS, BOOKLETS, AND SCRIPTURE PORTIONS
TO GIVE TO THE UNSAVED

These are among the best for Christians to give

to their unsaved friends to study as they consider the Saviour.

1. Graham, Billy: *Peace with God*: Affiliated Publishers, Inc., 630 Fifth Avenue, New York, New York 10020, 1953; 50¢.
2. Orr, J. Edwin. *Faith That Makes Sense*: The Judson Press, Valley Forge, Pa. 19481, 1960; $1.45.
3. Stott, J. R. W. *Basic Christianity*: Eerdmans Publishing Co., Grand Rapids, Michigan 49502, 1958; $1.25.
4. Strombeck, J. F. *Life That Is Eternal*: Good News Publishers, Westchester, Illinois 60155; 50¢.
5. Weiss, G. Christian. *On Being a Real Christian*: Good News Publishers, Westchester, Illinois 60155, 1964; 50¢.
6. "Becoming a Christian" by Stott: Inter-Varsity Press, 1519 N. Astor, Chicago, Illinois 60610, 1950; 15¢.
7. "Have You Considered Him?" by Smith: Inter-Varsity Press 1519 N. Astor, Chicago, Illinois 60610; 15¢.
8. "What Is Christianity?" by Weiss: Back to the Bible Publishers, Box 233, Lincoln, Nebraska 68501, 1958; 15¢.
9. *Gospel of John* with marked salvation verses (3 x 4¾): Pocket Testament League, 49 Honeck Street, Englewood, New York 07631; 8¢.
10. *Gospel of John* in Phillips Translation with pictures (5 x 7½): American Bible Society, 450 Park Avenue, New York, New York 10022; 15¢.
11. *Gospel of John* with extra large print (6 x 9¼): American Bible Society, 450 Park Avenue, New York, New York 10022; 28¢.
12. *Old Testament Prophecy Edition of the New Testament* (recommended for Jewish people): Million Testament Campaign, Inc., 1505 Race Street, Philadelphia, Pa. 19102; 75¢.

Tract Racks

These are helpful for placing Gospel literature in public places.

1. Metal tract rack, 2-pocket: American Tract Society, Oradell, New Jersey 07649; $1.50. With 200 tracts $2.50. Also 7-pocket for $7.50 ($10.00 with 700 tracts) and 12-pocket for $10.00 ($15.00 with 1200 tracts).
2. Wood tract rack, 6-pocket: Bethany Fellowship, Inc., 6820 Auto Club Road, Minneapolis, Minnesota 55431; $7.50. Also 15-pocket for $15.00.
3. Wood tract rack, 6-pocket: Good News Publishers, Westchester, Illinois 60155; $6.00. Also 15-pocket for $11.00 (with 1500 tracts $16.00).

Follow-up Materials for New Christians

Use these materials in effective follow-up of new Christians.

1. "Christ in You": Inter-Varsity Press, 1519 N. Astor, Chicago, Illinois 60610; 25¢ each.
2. "Established by the Word of God" by Coleman: Christian Outreach, Huntingdon Valley, Pennsylvania 19006, 1962; 40¢.
3. "How to Live for God!" by Smith: American Tract Society, Oradell, New Jersey 07649: 100 for $1.35.
4. "My Personal Bible Study": The Billy Graham Evangelistic Association, 1300 Harmon Place, Minneapolis, Minnesota 55403; 75¢ each (also other follow-up booklets).
5. "Studies in Christian Living": The Navigators, Colorado Springs, Colorado 80900; 45¢ for first booklet in series of 10 (also other follow-up booklets).

6. "Ten Basic Steps Toward Christian Maturity": Campus Crusade for Christ, Arrowhead Springs, San Bernardino, California 92400; 50¢ each, entire set of 11 for $4.40.

7. "The Light of Life Bible Correspondence Course": World Gospel Crusades, Box 42051, Los Angeles, California 90000; 25¢.

8. "Welcome to the Family of God" by Ford: American Tract Society, Oradell, New Jersey 07649; 100 for 90¢.

9. "What Christians Believe," Recorded Lecture Series, Vol. 1: Campus Crusade for Christ, Arrowhead Springs, San Bernardino, California 92400; 10–16⅔ RPM records, for $10.00.

Bible Reading, Study, and Memory Helps

These Bible reading, study, and memory helps and materials for personal and group use in continuous lay development are among the best to use, in conjunction with those listed in the sections on tracts on lay evangelism and lay evangelism training materials, to develop Christians into mature, effective, Christ-centered, Spirit-filled soul winners.

1. Items 4, 5, 6, and 9 above.

2. "Aldersgate Biblical Series" by various authors: Light and Life Press, Winona Lake, Indiana 46590.

3. "Growth by Groups" by Lyman Coleman: Christian Outreach, Huntingdon Valley, Pennsylvania 19006, 1962; 65¢.

4. "Life in the Living Word" by Coleman: Christian Outreach, Huntingdon Valley, Pennsylvania 19006, 1962; 65¢.

5. "The Spirit and the Word" by Coleman: Asbury Theological Seminary, Department of Evangelism, Wilmore, Kentucky 40390, 1965; 65¢.

6. "Through the Bible in a Year" by Flynn: American Tract Society, Oradell, New Jersey 07649; 100 for 90¢.
7. "Topical Memory System": The Navigators, Colorado Springs, Colorado 80900; $5.00.

BOOKS ON LAY WITNESSING

These books are highly recommended to give pastors and laymen the philosophy, challenge, and know-how of a church-related lay evangelism ministry.

1. Archibald, Arthur C. *New Testament Evangelism*: The Judson Press, Philadelphia, Pennsylvania 19481, 1946; $2.25.
2. Chafer, Lewis Sperry. *Winning Souls by Prayer*: Inter-Varsity Christian Fellowship, 1519 North Astor, Chicago, Illinois 60610, 1919; 15¢.
3. Coleman, Robert E. *The Master Plan of Evangelism*: Fleming H. Revell, Westwood, New Jersey 07675, 1963; $1.00.
4. Conant, J. E. *Every-Member Evangelism*: Harper and Row, Publishers, New York, New York 10016, 1922; $2.50.
5. Edwards, Gene. *How to Have a Soul-Winning Church*: Gospel Publishing House, 1445 Boonville Avenue, Springfield, Mo. 65802, 1963; $2.00.
6. Delamarter, George and Kingsley, Charles W. *Go*: Zondervan Publishing House, Grand Rapids, Michigan 49504, 1965; $1.50.
7. Krupp, Nate. *A World to Win*: Bethany Fellowship, Minneapolis, Minnesota 55431, 1966; $1.00.
8. *Evangelism in Depth* from Latin American Mission: Moody Press, Chicago, Illinois 60610, 1961; $2.25.
9. Monro, Rev. Claxton. *Witnessing Laymen Make Living Churches*: 1805 W. Alabama, Houston, Texas 77006, 1954; 20¢.

10. Moore, Waylon B. *New Testament Follow-up*: Wm. B. Eerdmans Company, Grand Rapids, Michigan 49502, 1963; $1.95.
11. Powell, Sidney W. *Fire on the Earth*: Broadman Press, Nashville, Tennessee 37203, 1963; $3.50.
12. Rees, Paul S. *Stir Up the Gift*: Zondervan Publishing House, Grand Rapids, Michigan 49504, 1952; $2.00.
13. Rinker, Rosalind. *You Can Witness with Confidence*: Zondervan Publishing House, Grand Rapids, Michigan 49504, 1962; $1.95.
14. Stewart, James A. *Evangelism*: Revival Literature, 1844–73rd Avenue, Philadelphia, Pennsylvania 19126, 1960.
15. Trotman, Dawson E. *Born to Reproduce*: Back to the Bible Publishers, Lincoln, Nebraska 68501, 1961; 10¢.
16. Trotman, Dawson E. *The Need of the Hour*: The Navigators, Colorado Springs, Colorado 80900, 1957; 15¢.
17. Trueblood, Elton. *The Company of the Committed*: Harper and Row, Publishers, New York New York 10016, 1961; $2.50.
18. Whitesell, Daniel Faris. *Basic New Testament Evangelism*: Zondervan Publishing House, Grand Rapids, Michigan 49504, 1949; $2.00.
19. Whitesell, Faris Daniel. *Great Personal Workers*: Moody Press, Chicago, Illinois 60610, 1956; 59¢.

BOOKS ON DISCIPLESHIP, PRAYER, REVIVAL, AND THE SPIRIT-FILLED LIFE

These books are among the best on the Spirit-filled life, etc.; so indispensable for successful soul winning.

1. An Unknown Christian. *The Power-Full Christian*: Zondervan Publishing House, Grand Rapids, Michigan 49504, 1961; $1.95.
2. Bounds, E. M. *Power Through Prayer*: Moody Press, Chicago, Illinois 60610; 15¢.
3. Geiger, Kenneth. *Insight Into Holiness*: Beacon Hill Press, Kansas City, Missouri 64141, 1962; $2.50.
4. Hall, Franklin. *The Fasting Prayer*: Franklin Hall, Box 11157, Phoenix, Arizona 85017, $2.00.
5. Hegre, T. A. *The Cross and Sanctification*: Bethany Fellowship, Minneapolis, Minnesota 55431, 1960; $2.75.
6. Hession, Roy. *The Calvary Road*: Christian Literature Crusade, Fort Washington, Pennsylvania 19034, 1950; 50¢.
7. Huegel, F. J. *Prayer's Deeper Secrets*: Zondervan Publishing House, Grand Rapids, Michigan 49504, 1959; $1.95.
8. MacDonald, William. *True Discipleship*: Midwest Christian Publishers, Box 453, Oak Park, Illinois 60300, 1962; 25¢.
9. McConkey, James H. *The Three-fold Secret of the Holy Spirit*: Moody Press, Chicago 60610, 1897; 39¢.
10. Nee, Watchman. *The Normal Christian Life*: Christian Literature Crusade, Fort Washington, Pennsylvania 19034, 1961; $1.25.
11. Olford, Stephen F. *Heart-Cry for Revival*: Fleming H. Revell Company, Westwood, New Jersey 07675, 1962; $2.50.
12. Orr, J. Edwin. *Full Surrender*: Marshall, Morgan & Scott, Ltd., London, England, 1951; $3.00.
13. Ravenhill, Leonard. *Why Revival Tarries*: Bethany Fellowship, Minneapolis, Minnesota 55431, 1959; $1.25.
14. Rinker, Rosalind. *Prayer, Conversing with God*:

Zondervan Publishing House, Grand Rapids, Michigan 49504, 1959; $1.95.

15. Shoemaker, Samuel M. *With the Holy Spirit and with Fire*: Harper & Row, Publishers, New York, New York 10016, 1960; $2.50.

16. Smith, Hannah Whitall. *The Christian's Secret of a Happy Life*: Fleming H. Revell Company, Westwood, New Jersey 07675, 1952; $1.00.

17. Thomas, Major W. Ian. *The Saving Life of Christ*: Zondervan Publishing House, Grand Rapids, Michigan 49504, 1961; $1.00.

18. Trumbull, Charles G. *Victory in Christ*: The Sunday School Times Company, 1211 Arch Street, Philadelphia, Pennsylvania 19105, 1959; 35¢.

ANTI-COMMUNIST BOOKS AND BOOKLETS

Although not directly related to lay evangelism, this list of some of the better anti-communist books has been added (1) because communism is one of the major contemporary threats to Christianity and (2) because mobilizing Christians to win souls is one of the few effective means of combating communism.

1. DeKoster, Lester. *Communism and Christian Faith*: Wm. B. Eerdmans Publishing Company, Grand Rapids, Michigan 49502, 1962; $3.50.

2. Ford, George L. *The Miracle of America*: Zondervan Publishing House, Grand Rapids, Michigan 49504, 1963; $1.00.

3. Hoover, J. Edgar. *Masters of Deceit*: Pocket Books, Inc., 630 Fifth Avenue, New York, New York 10020, 1958; 50¢.

4. Hoover, J. Edgar. *The Communist Menace*: Christianity Today, Washington Building, Washington, D.C. 20269; 10¢.

5. Montgomery, Joseph. *The Christian History of the Constitution*: The American Christian Press, San Francisco, California 94100, 1961; $7.50.
6. Neipp, Paul C. *Win Now or Lose All*: Parthenon Press, Nashville, Tennessee 37203, 1964; 25¢.
7. Noble, John. *I Found God in Soviet Russia*: St. Martin's Press, New York, New York 10000, 1959; $2.95.
8. Noble, John. *I Was a Slave in Russia*: Cicero Bible Press, Broadview, Illinois 60153, 1958; $1.00.
9. Schwarz, Dr. Fred. *You Can Trust the Communists*: Prentice-Hall, Inc., Englewood Cliffs, New Jersey 07631, 1960; $2.95.
10. Stormer, John A. *None Dare Call it Treason*: Liberty Bell Press, Box 32. Florissant, Missouri 63031, 1964; 75¢.

BOOKS ON MISSIONS

These challenging books on missions will give the reader a greater vision and burden to evangelize every creature in this generation.

1. Allen, Roland. *Missionary Methods—St. Paul's or Ours*: Wm. B. Eerdmans Company, Grand Rapids, Michigan 49502, 1962; $1.65.
2. Bailey, Faith Coxe. *Adoniram Judson*: Moody Press, Chicago, Illinois 60610; 39¢.
3. Davis, Walter B. *William Carey—Father of Modern Missions*: Moody Press, Chicago, Illinois 60610; $1.29.
4. Edwards, Jonathan. *The Life and Diary of David Brainerd*: Moody Press, Chicago, Illinois 60610; 89¢.
5. Elliot, Elisabeth. *Through Gates of Splendor*: Harper & Brothers, New York, New York 10016, 1957; $3.95.

6. Miller, Basil. *Praying Hyde*: Zondervan Publishing House, Grand Rapids, Michigan 49504; $1.95.

7. Smith, Oswald J. *The Passion for Souls*: Marshall, Morgan & Scott, Ltd., London, England.

8. Taylor, Mrs. Howard. *Bordon of Yale*: Moody Press, Chicago, Illinois; 89¢.

9. Taylor, Clyde W. *A Glimpse of World Missions*: Moody Press, Chicago, Illinois 60610; 1960; $1.00.

10. Taylor, J. Hudson. *A Retrospect*: Moody Press, Chicago, Illinois 60610; 59¢.

11. Wallis, Ethel E. and Bennet, Mary A. *Two Thousand Tongues to Go*: Harper and Brothers, New York, New York 10016, 1959; $3.95.

12. Worcester, Mrs. J. H., Jr. *David Livingstone*: Moody Press, Chicago, Illinois 60610; 39¢.

Appendix 3

DIRECTORY OF PERSONNEL IN PERSONAL EVANGELISM TRAINING WORK

Here is a list of those in full-time local-church-related personal evangelism training work. These individuals are all those known to the author at the time of publication to be in this type of ministry. The author would appreciate information of others for inclusion in later printings.

Archer, Mr. Vance: Director of Personal Evangelism, Methodist Church, 1908 Grand Avenue, Nashville, Tennessee 37205.

Bassett, Mr. Bud: Field Director, Shalom, Box 3317, Merchandise Mart Station, Chicago, Illinois 60600.

Bright, Dr. William R.: Director, Campus Crusade for Christ, International, Arrowhead Springs, San Bernardino, California 92400.

Coleman, Rev. Lyman: Executive Secretary, Christian Outreach, Box 115, Huntingdon Valley, Pennsylvania 19006.

Cook, Rev. Luther T.: House-to-House Visitation, 517 Jefferson Street, Woodstock, Illinois 60098.

Curry, Mr. Ray: Personal Evangelist, R.D. 5, Meadville, Pennsylvania 16335.

Elmore, Rev. Lee E.: Personal Evangelist, 2015 Sibley Street, St. Charles, Missouri 63301.

Evangelism in Depth: Latin America Mission, 285 Orchard Terrace, Bogota, New Jersey 07603.

Funk, Rev. Abe: Director, God's Invasion Army, 5750 North Ashland Avenue, Chicago, Illinois 60628.

Harris, Rev. James: Jim Harris Evangelistic Association, Box 6133, Seattle, Washington 98100.

Holden, Rev. William: Director, House-to-House Visitation Evangelism, 607 Kent Avenue, Teaneck, New Jersey 07666.

Hurt, Rev. Robert: Director, America Evangelistic Association, Box 5205, St. Paul, Minnesota 55104.

Kingsley, Rev. Charles W.: Executive Director, Light and Life Men's Fellowship, Free Methodist Church, Spring Arbor, Michigan 49283.

Krupp, Mr. Nate: Director, Lay Evangelism, Inc., Box 565, Wheaton, Illinois 60187.

Lovett, Rev. Cummings S.: Director, Personal Christianity, Box 157, Baldwin Park, California 91760.

Matthews, Rev. Elwood: Church of God of Prophecy, Bible Place, Cleveland, Tennessee 37311.

Mitchell, Rev. Hubert: Director, Inter-Church Ministries, 77 W. Washington Street, Chicago, Illinois 60602.

Petrehn, Mr. John: Personal Evangelist, 5100 Howe Drive, Shawnee Mission, Kansas.

Pierce, Rev. Burton W.: National Secretary of Men's Fellowship, Assemblies of God, 1445 Boonville Avenue, Springfield, Missouri 65802.

Rinker, Miss Rosalind: Author and Lecturer, 2120 North Lincoln Park West, Chicago, Illinois 60600.

Sanny, Mr. Lorne: President, The Navigators, Box 1861, Colorado Springs, Colorado 80900.

Whipple, Mr. Leonard: Personal Evangelist, 4549 ½ Auhay Drive, Santa Barbara, California 93105.

Appendix 4

REFERENCES

1. Hegre, T. A., *The Cross and Sanctification*: Minneapolis, Bethany Fellowship, Inc., 1960, p. 263.
2. Whitesell, F. D., *Basic New Testament Evangelism*: Grand Rapids, Zondervan Publishing House, 1949, pp. 107 ff.
3. *Ibid.*, p. 112.
4. Archibald, Arthur C., *New Testament Evangelism*: Philadelphia, The Judson Press, 1946, p. 44.
5. Shoemaker, Samuel M., *With the Holy Spirit and with Fire*: New York, Harper & Row, Publishers, 1960, p. 88.
6. Conant, J. E., *Every-Member Evangelism*: New York, Harper & Row, Publishers, 1922, p. 31.
7. Report from Interdenominational Foreign Mission Association "Congress on World Missions" December 1960.
8. Edwards, Gene, *How to Have a Soul-Winning Church*: Soul Winning Publications, 1962, p. 35.
9. Conant, J. E., *Op. cit.*, p. 31.
10. Torrey, R. A., *How to Work for Christ*: Westwood, Fleming H. Revell Company, pp. 9 ff.
11. Edwards, Gene, *Op. cit.*, p. 27.
12. Conant, J. E., *Op. cit.*, pp. 22 ff.
13. *Ibid.* pp. 54 ff.

Every effort has been made to secure permission from authors and publishers for quoted materials. Additional acknowledgment is made to the following: Archibald, Arthur. *New Testament Evangelism*: Valley Forge, Pennsylvania, The Judson Press; Coleman, Robert. *The Master Plan of Evangelism*: Wilmore, Kentucky, Asbury Theological Seminary; Conant, J. E. *Every-Member Evangelism*: New York,

N.Y., Harper & Row Publishers; Dean, Horace. *Visitation Evangelism Made Practical*: Grand Rapids, Michigan, Zondervan Publishing House; *Evangelism in Depth*: Chicago, Illinois, Moody Press, Moody Bible Institute; Monro, Claxton. *Witnessing Laymen Make Living Churches,* Houston, Texas; Moore, Waylon B. *New Testament Follow-up for Pastors and Laymen*: Grand Rapids, Michigan, Wm. B. Eerdmans Publishing Co.; Raines, Robert A. *New Life in the Church*: New York, N.Y., Harper & Row Publishers; Ravenhill, Leonard. *Why Revival Tarries*: Minneapolis, Minnesota, Bethany Fellowship; Rees, Paul S. *Stir Up the Gift*: Grand Rapids, Michigan, Zondervan Publishing House; Rinker, Rosalind. *Yau Can Witness with Confidence*: Grand Rapids, Michigan, Zondervan Publishing House; Shoemaker, Samuel. *With the Holy Spirit and with Fire*: New York, N.Y., Harper & Row Publishers; Stewart, James A. *Evangelism*: Chattanooga, Tennessee, Revival Literature; Sweeting, George. *"Communism or Christ"*: Oradell, New Jersey, American Tract Society; Trotman, Dawson, *The Need of the Hour*: Colorado Springs, Colorado, The Navigators; Trueblood, Elton. *The Company of the Committed*: New York, N.Y., Harper & Row Publishers; Whitesell, F. D. *Basic New Testament Evangelism*: Grand Rapids, Michigan, Zondervan Publishing House.